Think Like an Owner

Think Like an Owner

Mindsets that drive long-term financial success

Julian Hawthorne

Mindful Pages

Published in 2025

ISBN: 9789371778206 (PB)
ISBN: 9789371776752 (eBook)

Published by

Mindful Pages
Imprint of Alpha Editions LLC
312 W. 2nd St #1834
Casper, WY 82601, USA

This book was developed using advanced writing tools to support the drafting and ideation process. All content has been thoughtfully curated, refined, and reviewed to ensure quality and relevance.

Content

Introduction
The Hidden Architecture of Wealth

Wealth is often judged by what is immediately visible: the figures on a bank statement, the assets tallied on a spreadsheet, the square footage of a property, or the accolades that signal status. Yet beneath this surface lies a far subtler, far more decisive structure—a hidden framework that determines not just how wealth is acquired, but how it is sustained, leveraged, and passed on. This book delves into that framework. It is concerned not simply with the mechanics of investing or the discipline of budgeting, but with the unseen scaffolding of beliefs, behaviours, and mental models that quietly govern our financial lives.

Here, ownership is not a line on a title deed or a note in a shareholder register. It is not conferred by banks, legal instruments, or tax codes. Ownership is a lens, a mode of decision-making, and a form of stewardship. It is a state of mind. And it is this mindset—not technical skill alone—that separates those who prosper over decades from those buffeted by markets, moods, or fleeting distractions.

The central thesis of *Think Like an Owner* is both simple and profound: long-term financial success hinges less on knowledge than on thought patterns—and even more on how one behaves under pressure, uncertainty, and opportunity. This mindset is not innate. It is cultivated, deliberately chosen, and accessible to anyone willing to examine themselves as rigorously as they study the world around them.

Why Ownership Is a Way of Being

True ownership begins where entitlement ends. It demands an acceptance of responsibility that transcends control, extending into vision. To own fully—whether it is a business, a body of work, a portfolio, or a set of values—is to regard it not merely as property, but as an ongoing project of significance. It requires foresight, emotional resilience, and the humility to recognise that while we can steer the ship, we do not command the sea.

Financially, this perspective runs counter to the prevailing culture of short-termism. Ownership asks: What am I creating that will endure? It shifts focus from extraction to cultivation, from immediacy to sustainability. This is not sentimental; it is strategic. Those who approach wealth as a game to be won often burn out or break down. Those who nurture it as a garden, season by season, decade by decade, leave a legacy that persists.

Systems thinkers have long observed that outcomes in complex processes are determined more by underlying structures than by surface actions—by incentives, feedback loops, and mental models. Financial life is no different. Ownership, in this sense, is the invisible system behind visible results. It is the distinction between reacting to markets and shaping one's own economy; between wishing for financial independence and constructing it deliberately.

The Myth of the Intelligent Investor

We idolise the notion of the "brilliant investor"—the individual with rare insight, unshakable discipline, and enviable returns. Yet intelligence alone rarely predicts sustained success. History is littered with brilliant minds undone by overconfidence, impatience, or identity misalignment.

The myth persists because it flatters our desire to feel exceptional. But the evidence, especially from longitudinal studies, tells a humbler tale: long-term financial achievement depends not on genius, but on consistency, self-awareness, and the patience to see through decades. The differentiators are internal infrastructure: identity, values, emotional fluency, and the ability to defer gratification in service of something larger.

That "something larger" is not wealth accumulation for its own sake. It is wealth integration—the transformation of money into a tool of freedom rather than a measure of self-worth or shame. Thinking like an owner means aligning capital with purpose, using it to amplify values, and recognising that the most powerful investments are those made in how one lives, not merely what one buys.

From Hustle to Stewardship

Our culture celebrates hustle, speed, and visibility, often shaming slowness. But activity without direction is a liability. The chase for more—more income, more recognition, more efficiency—has left many financially busy yet spiritually impoverished. "Getting ahead" becomes an empty refrain unless we ask: ahead of what? For whose sake? At what cost?

Hustle, in its modern guise, is often reactive: a compensation for feelings of inadequacy or scarcity. Money becomes a finish line rather than a medium of stewardship. Stewardship reframes the conversation. It acknowledges that wealth is not solely for saving or spending, but for shaping the world intentionally. True ownership is a practice of long-term care: thinking in decades, even generations, rather than quarters; resisting short-term wins to honour the compounding power of deliberate effort.

What This Book Offers

Finance literature is abundant, filled with guides to investing, budgeting hacks, side hustles, and FIRE strategies. Scarcer are works that explore money as terrain of psychology, philosophy, and cultural inheritance. *Think Like an Owner* occupies that space.

This is not a manual of tactics. It is a mental operating system for wealth. It offers no formulas, only frameworks—tested across disciplines, histories, and lived experience—that allow readers to perceive money through a more powerful lens. You will not be told which stocks to buy or when to time markets. Instead, you will learn to select enduring principles, train attention, and design a life that does not rely on luck or spectacle.

Insights are drawn from behavioural economics, indigenous wisdom, investment philosophy, family governance, and trauma-informed finance. You will encounter concepts such as emotional liquidity, return on attention, psychological portfolio management, and generational stewardship—not as abstractions, but as practices with tangible impact.

Above all, this book bridges external wealth and internal capacity. It addresses the questions that arise after debt is repaid, businesses established, or income thresholds crossed: Now what? What does all this signify? Who am I, when survival is no longer the primary objective, and purpose becomes the guiding principle?

An Invitation to a Different Kind of Wealth

This book is for those who sense that conventional financial advice is incomplete. It speaks to the successful who remain unfulfilled, to beginners aware that much is left unsaid. Entrepreneurs, investors, creatives, parents, and professionals alike—anyone seeking coherence, autonomy, and legacy—will find resonance here.

Thinking like an owner transcends mere accumulation. It is about becoming whole. It aligns financial life with values, time with priorities, and decisions with one's future self. It shifts from reactive consumerism to the quiet confidence of strategic stewardship.

This book does not pander or shortcut growth. It asks readers to slow down, challenge assumptions, and reclaim authorship of their financial narrative. For those willing to think in systems rather than outcomes, wealth becomes not a pursuit, but a creation from the inside out.

In the chapters ahead, you will explore how identity shapes investment, how culture scripts financial patterns, and how time itself can be transformed from constraint into resource. Ownership is framed not as a destination, but as a deliberate, decisive way of moving through life.

This is your invitation: not to master money, but to master your relationship with it; not to compete for status, but to surpass the limits of reactive living. The path is one of conscious design, not blind optimisation. It is not about winning the game, but redefining its purpose.

Welcome to the hidden architecture of wealth. Let us begin.

Chapter 1
The Owner's Mind

Ownership is frequently misunderstood in contemporary culture. It is often mistaken for control, conflated with possession, and cheapened by the language of entitlement. Yet the kind of ownership we explore here is different—profoundly so. It is neither a legal document nor a balance sheet entry; it is a mental framework, a philosophy of agency, a disciplined alignment of thought and action. The owner's mind does not obsess over grasping, guarding, or micromanaging. Instead, it is anchored in vision, resilience, and the ability to influence outcomes without trying to command every variable. This chapter delves into that mindset. We will examine the fine line between controlling something and truly owning it, uncover how identity silently scaffolds financial behaviour, consider time as a strategic asset rather than a mere schedule, and reveal the hidden cost of living according to a culture of consumption rather than one of investment.

The distinction between ownership and control is fundamental. Control is reactive; it springs from fear—fear of loss, failure, or uncertainty. It drives the compulsion to micromanage, to anticipate every contingency, to eliminate risk entirely. In doing so, it creates the illusion of power while fostering fragility. Ownership, in contrast, is proactive. It acknowledges the inevitability of change and aligns with it. Strategic, adaptive, patient—true ownership cultivates influence not through domination of every detail, but through systems designed to endure. Consider the entrepreneur who builds a business that thrives without constant oversight versus the founder who cannot sleep unless every transaction is supervised. The difference is instructive.

Ironically, the more one clings to control, the less one experiences real ownership. Control delivers immediacy but remains brittle; ownership unfolds slowly yet endures. The owner asks not, "How do I prevent this from breaking today?" but rather, "What structure will still be standing in a decade?" This distinction applies to finances, organisations, relationships, and even the inner life.

Control seeks outcomes; ownership seeks alignment. Control craves certainty; ownership cultivates direction.

Such an orientation requires an invisible inner infrastructure. Each of us carries a psychological portfolio—a constellation of beliefs, fears, reflexive emotions, and inherited narratives that quietly govern our approach to money, risk, time, and self-worth. Some elements are explicit: lessons absorbed from mentors, mantras internalised through reading or schooling. Many are subterranean: family dynamics, cultural expectations, early encounters with scarcity or abundance. Together, they form the operating system beneath our financial decisions—what we notice, ignore, rationalise, or evade.

Take, for instance, the belief that money must be earned through struggle. Admirable at first glance—discipline, sacrifice, effort—but unexamined, it can become a bottleneck, leading one to avoid opportunities that arrive with ease or to resist delegation even when it would multiply value. Or the fear of being seen as selfish for seeking wealth, manifesting as chronic underpricing, over-giving, or neglecting personal development. Spreadsheets cannot fix these patterns. They demand excavation, reflection, and rewiring. To think like an owner is to manage not just assets, but the internal narratives that shape them.

Psychological portfolio management is central to the ideas that follow. Just as financial portfolios require diversification, stress-testing, and periodic rebalancing, so too must our internal architecture. Beliefs that served us in one phase of life may hinder us in another. Identities forged in scarcity may obstruct growth in abundance. Ownership demands the courage to audit not only accounts but assumptions.

Identity is thus infrastructure, not description. It sets the ceiling for financial life long before strategy enters the frame. A steward thinks differently than a spender, a hustler, or a perpetual underdog. The steward asks, "What am I responsible for sustaining and passing on?" The spender asks, "What can I enjoy right now?" The hustler asks, "How do I stay ahead?" None are inherently wrong—but only one is designed for continuity.

The owner's identity is built for time, not merely for longevity, but for strategic duration. Time itself is a misunderstood asset. Modernity teaches us to slice it, optimise it, monetise it—a treatment inherited from industrial-age thinking that misses a deeper truth: time is a dimension of meaning.

There is a difference between thinking in hours and thinking in epochs. Founders of enduring institutions, builders of intergenerational wealth, and elders in traditional societies understand that time exists in layers. There is clock time—the schedules, deadlines, and immediacy of action. And there is kairos—the opportune moment, the right rhythm, the patience to wait for ripeness. Ownership lives in this second register. It is deliberate, unhurried, attuned. Timing, not merely speed, is a form of intelligence.

Consider someone viewing a career in quarterly performance versus one who builds legacies. The former chases promotions, visibility, and immediate wins; the latter cultivates reputation, nurtures relationships, and prioritises positioning over transient results. Similarly, in investing, traders seek volatility; owners seek compounding. One plays games of precision, the other plays games of duration. Ownership is not inertia; it is strategically patient.

This temporal lens illuminates the hidden cost of consumer culture. Modern economies thrive on attention extraction and instant gratification. We are encouraged to consume not to fulfil needs, but to construct identities. Purchases become proxies for self-worth; experiences become curated performances rather than sources of meaning. Agency quietly erodes. We cease choosing and begin reacting. Consumption becomes both financial and existential.

A consumer mindset flattens time and narrows perspective. It fosters addiction to novelty, diminishes discernment, and seduces us into mistaking stimulation for satisfaction. Beneath this lies a deeper consequence: the erosion of sovereignty, accumulation of unseen debt—emotional, psychological, relational—and the surrender of future options to present distraction.

To reclaim ownership is to reject this default mode. Every financial decision carries not only monetary cost but narrative consequence. Each purchase either reinforces or undermines the story you wish to inhabit. Each investment is a vote for the world you want to live in. Ownership asks: Does this choice align with who I am becoming? Control asks: Will it prevent something bad? One builds orientation; the other breeds anxiety.

In this chapter, we will explore these ideas in depth. Real-world examples will illustrate entrepreneurs who designed ventures resilient beyond their lifetimes, families who transmitted values more than money, investors who achieved wealth through behavioural mastery rather than chasing returns. We will examine internal architecture—how childhood experiences shape adult strategies, how emotion affects decisions under uncertainty, and how time mirrors values.

Ultimately, the owner's mind is defined not by what it knows, but by how it perceives. Money becomes a medium of stewardship, risk something to be calibrated, time an arena in which meaning unfolds.

This is the shift we undertake: from reactive control to proactive ownership; from unconscious consumption to intentional construction; from chasing wealth to designing systems that generate it—over years, decades, and generations.

Welcome to the owner's mind. The work of thinking in alignment with what truly endures begins here.

The Difference Between Ownership and Control

One of the most overlooked distinctions in the psychology of success is the difference between ownership and control. On the surface, the two may appear interchangeable—both imply authority, involvement, decision-making power. But beneath the surface, they diverge sharply. Control is often rooted in fear. Ownership, in contrast, is rooted in vision. Control micromanages; ownership designs. Control tightens its grip as uncertainty rises; ownership expands its frame to accommodate complexity. One constricts. The other creates.

Understanding this difference is not an academic exercise—it is foundational to whether we build durable wealth, sustainable systems, or brittle illusions of security. Professionals who conflate the two often find themselves exhausted, perpetually reactive, and trapped in a loop of diminishing returns. Those who learn to differentiate—and choose ownership—gain something much rarer: leverage, clarity, and resilience.

Control seeks predictability. It operates from the premise that if everything is monitored closely enough, risk can be eliminated. This instinct is understandable. We live in a world that equates control with competence. But competence without perspective becomes fragility. Micromanagement, whether in financial planning or leadership, is not a strength—it is a symptom of mistrust. And over time, it suffocates initiative, blinds us to opportunity, and creates systems that collapse when the controller steps away.

By contrast, ownership does not require omniscience. It assumes variability and plans accordingly. Owners ask different questions. Not "What can I prevent from going wrong today?" but "What systems can I build that continue to function—even flourish—when I am no longer directly involved?" This is not a hands-off philosophy. It is a design-oriented one. It demands deep engagement at the level of principles, structure, and foresight, not perpetual interference in the mechanics.

Consider the difference between a founder who insists on signing off every purchase order and one who invests in training, values alignment, and culture-building so that their team makes wise decisions autonomously. The former may achieve temporary precision. The latter builds scale. Ownership is a long game. It trusts in the compounding effects of clarity, delegation, and well-defined systems.

This distinction plays out with striking clarity in financial behaviour. Many individuals who are highly educated and professionally successful still operate financially from a control mindset. They track every transaction obsessively, second-guess every decision, and react to market swings with disproportionate anxiety. Their financial lives are technically active but emotionally passive—driven by fear of loss rather than confidence in direction.

True financial ownership, by contrast, looks very different. It begins with a framework—defining values, time horizon, risk appetite, and desired outcomes. It requires a macro perspective: allocating capital not for maximum short-term gain, but for alignment with personal or familial objectives. It allows for fluctuations, unexpected expenses, even downturns—because the owner has already built a structure that accounts for imperfection. Control aims for precision. Ownership designs for robustness.

There is a cultural element to this dichotomy as well. Western capitalist societies have long valorised the image of the controlling leader: the CEO who works 90-hour weeks, the investor who outsmarts the market, the parent who choreographs every detail of a child's life. But beneath this idealisation is often a deep fragility. The controlling leader burns out. The outsmarting investor misses black swan events. The over-parented child becomes risk-averse and dependent. Control, taken too far, hollows out the very autonomy and adaptability we claim to value.

Ownership, though less glamorous on the surface, is far more powerful in practice. It is not about being in charge of everything; it is about being responsible for the outcomes of everything you touch. It is a quiet discipline—deeply unsexy, often invisible. But it creates environments in which other people, capital, and ideas can thrive without constant supervision. It is the operating mode of great investors, resilient founders, and high-functioning families. And it can be cultivated.

The transition from control to ownership requires a psychological shift—a movement from scarcity to strategy. Control operates from the belief that things must be held tightly or they will fall apart. Ownership understands that most things fall apart because they were never built to function without constant intervention. This distinction is visible in everything from organisational design to personal finance to how we relate to our time.

Take, for example, time management. Control-based thinkers obsess over time blocks, productivity tools, and squeezing efficiency from every hour. The result is often increased stress and a perpetual sense of insufficiency. The owner's approach is different: time is not merely managed; it is allocated according to values and intention. The owner designs their week to reflect priorities, not just obligations. They recognise that not all hours are equal. Some produce insight. Others produce noise. Ownership is about making those distinctions with clarity and conviction.

The same pattern appears in investment philosophy. The controller trades frequently, chases trends, and tries to outmanoeuvre markets. The owner builds a portfolio aligned with long-term objectives and lets it compound. One is exhausting. The other is effective. Studies consistently show that the best performing retail investors are not the ones who check their portfolios daily, but those who forget their login credentials for years. The lesson is clear: more control does not equal more return. Often, it reduces it.

But perhaps the most overlooked domain in which this distinction matters is emotional regulation. Control-based behaviour is typically an emotional management strategy. It tries to reduce anxiety by increasing oversight. But it rarely works. The more we try to control what cannot be controlled—markets, people, external validation—the more anxious we become. Ownership flips this dynamic. It accepts uncertainty and focuses on what can be designed, influenced, or prepared for. It reallocates emotional energy from surveillance to strategy.

Real-world examples illustrate this powerfully. Consider the approach of Yvon Chouinard, founder of Patagonia. He deliberately built an ownership culture—one that empowered employees, prioritised long-term environmental impact over short-term profits, and embedded sustainability into every process. He could have maintained tighter personal control. Instead, he ceded ownership entirely, placing the company into a purpose trust so that profits would permanently serve the planet. That is ownership in its purest form: influence without interference, vision over vigilance.

Another example is Jeff Bezos's strategic concept of "disagree and commit," often misunderstood as a tactical tool but fundamentally a philosophy of ownership. It assumes that decisions will not always be made with unanimous agreement, but that trust in the system, and clarity of roles, allows progress to continue. Micromanagers require consensus because they fear letting go. Owners cultivate resilience by enabling others to act within clearly defined parameters.

Control, when left unchecked, breeds stagnation. It creates environments where people wait for instructions rather than take initiative, where organisations are paralysed by over-dependence on a single decision-maker. Ownership, by contrast, fosters antifragility. It distributes authority through trust and clarity, creating systems that improve through use and stress rather than deteriorate.

There are, of course, moments when control is necessary. Emergencies demand it. High-stakes decisions occasionally require command-level involvement. But the problem arises when control becomes the default mode. Like a powerful drug, it may bring short-term relief but long-term dependence. Ownership, while slower to implement, offers immunity. It builds capacity in others, strength in systems, and clarity in strategy.

The transition is not merely behavioural—it is existential. It requires a willingness to let go of the ego rewards of control: being needed, being the smartest person in the room, being central to every decision. Ownership, paradoxically, often means becoming less visible. But what it sacrifices in proximity, it gains in influence. To own something well is to no longer need to constantly prove that you own it.

For professionals, the implications are far-reaching. A manager who builds autonomous teams becomes more valuable, not less. A founder who systematises their company increases its worth. A family that passes on principles, not just money, leaves a deeper legacy. Control may generate temporary stability, but ownership creates institutional memory, cultural coherence, and structural longevity.

This is the shift this book invites: from nervous micromanagement to confident design. From scarcity-rooted control to system-rooted ownership. From needing to be everywhere to knowing that what you've built can operate without you. Ownership is not about letting go of excellence—it is about changing the location of your effort. Not at the edge of every detail, but at the centre of every structure.

The best owners are not those who hold on tightest, but those who build what can endure without them. Their influence grows as their control decreases. Their legacy expands as their grip loosens. Not because they care less, but because they have learned to care wisely.

That is the difference between ownership and control. And it is the difference between building something that thrives, and something that merely survives.

Identity as Financial Infrastructure

Most financial models begin with numbers. They work outward from income, expenses, investment vehicles, and tax structures. But these models—however technically sound—are downstream of something far more formative: identity. Before we save, spend, invest, or budget, we *believe.* We *interpret.* We *react.* These internal dynamics form the invisible infrastructure upon which all our financial outcomes rest. Identity is not merely a philosophical abstraction; it is a material force. It determines how risk feels, what enough looks like, and where we unconsciously cap our potential. To understand money behaviour without understanding identity is to treat symptoms while ignoring their root system.

The premise here is both radical and intuitive: our financial lives are not built primarily by market conditions, economic policy, or luck. They are built by internal architecture—beliefs formed early, shaped by family scripts, reinforced by cultural narratives, and silently repeated through daily decisions. We tend to think of identity as fixed, or at best cosmetic. In reality, it functions more like a psychological operating system—setting parameters, issuing silent commands, and determining the quality of decisions we make over time.

Begin with a simple but revealing observation: two people with similar incomes, similar access to information, and similar levels of intelligence can—and routinely do—end up with vastly different financial realities. One accumulates and sustains wealth with a sense of purpose. The other cycles through gains and losses with no lasting progress. The difference, more often than not, is not strategy. It is identity. One sees themselves as a steward of long-term value. The other may unconsciously view money as unsafe, shameful, or temporary. And these self-concepts do not remain abstract. They translate into action: how often we check our investments, how we respond to downturns, how much we trust ourselves to make high-stakes choices.

The field of financial therapy has begun to codify this relationship, identifying what are often called "money scripts"—core beliefs formed in childhood that shape adult financial behaviour. These scripts often operate below conscious awareness. A person who heard "money doesn't grow on trees" during formative years may grow up to become chronically risk-averse or overly frugal, even when financially secure. Another who absorbed the idea that "you have to spend to enjoy life" may struggle to build reserves, constantly converting income into status or sensory experience. These scripts are not irrational—they are adaptive. They once served a purpose. But over time, if left unexamined, they harden into constraints.

This is why identity is not just a psychological curiosity—it is infrastructure. It determines the ceiling of what is financially possible long before we encounter real-world variables. A client earning £200,000 per year but internally tethered to the belief that wealth makes you morally suspect will eventually find ways to self-sabotage—through over-giving, under-investing, or unconsciously aligning with volatile partners or causes. The external income matters little if the internal permission structure is not upgraded.

The idea of *psychological portfolio management* emerges from this insight. Just as we diversify financial portfolios to manage volatility and optimise returns, we must also examine and recalibrate the beliefs and identities that govern our financial decisions. This process is not esoteric; it is practical. It begins by identifying the dominant scripts we operate from—whether inherited, reactive, or aspirational—and assessing their current utility. A belief that helped you survive your twenties may prevent you from thriving in your forties. A family narrative that once bonded generations may now be constraining initiative and experimentation. The goal is not to discard identity wholesale, but to consciously evolve it.

Consider the distinction between a consumer identity and an owner identity. The consumer is validated by spending, visibility, and lifestyle optics. The owner is oriented toward stewardship, value creation, and long-term coherence. These are not mere labels. They are behavioural blueprints. The consumer may feel a surge of pride when making a luxury purchase, associating it with success or arrival. The owner may feel satisfaction not in the purchase, but in the alignment of that purchase with larger goals. One is reactive. The other is generative.

This is not a moral distinction; it is a structural one. Systems built on consumption require constant inputs and tend to be fragile in downturns. Systems built on ownership tend to be more resilient, capable of compounding, and less emotionally volatile. And because identity shapes what we notice, these systems end up shaping what opportunities we perceive. The person who sees themselves as a builder looks for patterns. The one who sees themselves as a hustler looks for breaks. The builder may play a longer game with fewer dopamine hits. But over time, they end up with equity—in finances, relationships, and reputation.

The role of family dynamics here cannot be overstated. Many of our financial identities are not individually chosen but intergenerationally inherited. We learn not only through explicit instruction, but through modelling. A parent who refused to discuss money may have communicated that financial matters are shameful or dangerous. A family that associated wealth with corruption may raise children who unconsciously disown ambition. These legacies shape our baseline expectations—what we think we deserve, how we respond to abundance, and whether we see financial independence as a right, a privilege, or a threat.

What complicates this further is that many of these patterns are culturally reinforced. In some communities, financial success is associated with betrayal—of one's roots, one's people, or one's values. In others, it may be seen as a form of personal validation, proof that one has "made it." Both interpretations come with psychological costs. The former may produce guilt or invisibility. The latter can breed perfectionism or performative success. Neither allows for fluid, integrated growth. The work of psychological portfolio management involves disentangling these narratives, updating them, and anchoring financial choices in values that are consciously selected rather than unconsciously inherited.

Real-world cases illustrate the impact of this work. A tech executive in his forties discovers that despite earning more than he ever imagined, he feels persistently anxious. Upon exploration, it becomes clear that his sense of safety is tied not to his actual net worth but to his father's early bankruptcy, which he witnessed as a teenager. His identity remains structured around loss-prevention, not value creation. Only by naming this architecture—and updating it—can he begin to take measured risks that align with his actual context. Another example: a woman who grew up in a family where generosity was equated with virtue finds herself unable to say no to financial requests from relatives, even when they undermine her goals. Her identity is loyal, sacrificial, and deeply embedded in belonging. But it is not aligned with ownership. Reclaiming agency requires not just financial boundaries, but identity revision.

The academic literature supports this view. Behavioural economics has long shown that individuals do not act rationally with money; they act narratively. We are, as the economist Robert Shiller put it, *storytelling animals*, and the stories we tell ourselves about money—what it means, what it says about us, what it allows or forbids—are more determinative than most budgets or balance sheets. The psychologist Carol Dweck's work on mindset further reinforces this: a fixed identity around money ("I'm bad with finances") leads to avoidance, while a growth identity ("I'm learning to steward capital wisely") creates momentum and curiosity.

But awareness alone is insufficient. Integration requires consistent reflection, exposure to alternative models, and often, relational reinforcement. This is why coaching, therapy, and intentional peer groups can be so effective. They do not merely offer advice—they challenge and expand identity. They provide mirrors and maps. They help individuals reauthor the financial narratives they live by.

For professionals seeking to become true owners—not merely earners, spenders, or savers—this work is indispensable. Financial planning without identity work is like constructing a building on uncertain soil. No matter how elegant the architecture, the foundation will fail under pressure. But when identity is clarified—when beliefs align with values, and narratives support rather than sabotage behaviour—decisions become cleaner. Risk becomes less threatening. Growth becomes less accidental and more directional.

The most successful individuals in any field tend to have one thing in common: not just technical mastery, but psychological congruence. Their external choices reflect an internal clarity. They know who they are, what they value, and what trade-offs they are willing to make. This clarity is not a fixed state—it is maintained through conscious attention, just like any well-managed portfolio. It is regularly reviewed, stress-tested, and adjusted. The result is not perfection but alignment. And alignment, when sustained over time, produces results that no external system can replicate.

Identity is not a soft variable. It is the hard surface upon which all financial tools land. It shapes what feels risky, what feels safe, what feels right. It can sabotage our plans or supercharge our progress. If left unexamined, it governs us. But if brought into consciousness, it can be reshaped—transformed from a silent constraint into a strategic asset.

That is the work of the owner: not just to optimise cash flow, but to steward identity. Not just to build a portfolio of assets, but to manage the architecture of belief that determines how those assets are used. The owner knows that financial independence is not a finish line—it is a reflection of internal coherence. And that coherence begins not with better tools, but with a clearer self.

The Inner Game of Time

Nothing reveals the depth of one's ownership mindset more than their relationship to time. It is the most democratically distributed resource—twenty-four hours for every human being on the planet—yet it is used with wildly uneven results. Some people treat time as a conveyor belt they're frantically trying to keep up with. Others use it as a canvas—selecting carefully what to place where, and with what intention. This distinction is not primarily about productivity techniques. It is about time perception. More specifically, it is about *temporal orientation*—the mental model through which one relates to time as a strategic variable rather than a background condition. Owners think in decades. Operators think in days.

The financial industry, particularly in its corporate form, has taught us to think in quarters—ninety-day performance windows that compress judgement and penalise patience. But legacy is never built quarterly. Vision does not conform to calendar earnings cycles. Founders who create institutions that outlive them, and stewards who compound value across generations, operate on a different temporal wavelength. They are not racing the clock. They are aligning with it. Their strength is not in speed, but in discernment—knowing when to act decisively and when to wait, even when the market clamours for immediacy.

This is not to romanticise slowness for its own sake. Urgency has its place. But when urgency becomes the default lens, it erodes strategic capacity. Decisions made under constant time pressure often collapse into risk-aversion or impulsivity. What is needed instead is what indigenous traditions and enduring founder philosophies have long understood: *time is not linear, but layered.* It is not merely what passes; it is what unfolds. To engage in the inner game of time is to shift from managing time reactively to shaping it deliberately.

The Potawatomi scholar and botanist Robin Wall Kimmerer speaks of time in indigenous cultures as something far more relational than Western models permit. In *Braiding Sweetgrass*, she writes of calendars that follow ecological events—like the bloom of a certain flower or the return of migratory birds—not arbitrary months. Time, in these systems, is observed through relationship and readiness, not through rigidity. You act when the earth signals it's time. This sensibility has profound implications for ownership. It teaches us that timing is contextual intelligence. And it reminds us that growth follows rhythms we cannot force but must learn to work with.

Modern founders who think like owners often carry this same intuition, whether or not they name it as such. Consider the case of Jim Collins's concept of the "20 Mile March," derived from his study of companies that thrived across economic cycles. The consistent characteristic? Pacing. The best leaders didn't sprint when times were good and collapse when times were lean. They moved with strategic consistency, resisting the temptation to overextend or underperform. They understood that the discipline of pacing beats the drama of performance spikes. Their relationship to time was not about intensity, but intentionality.

There is a stark difference between being busy and being aligned. The former is a temporal addiction; the latter is a temporal philosophy. To think like an owner is to detach from the false urgency of constant output and anchor oneself in durable priorities. This means learning to differentiate between *chronos* and *kairos*—two ancient Greek concepts of time that continue to offer startling relevance.

Chronos refers to sequential, measurable time: hours, minutes, deadlines. It is the domain of schedules and systems. *Kairos*, by contrast, denotes the opportune moment—the qualitative time when something is ripe for action. It is what a seasoned investor senses when entering a position that others overlook. It is what a great leader recognises when timing a pivot or a public message. The owner respects *chronos* but moves according to *kairos*. They do not confuse action with progress, nor do they mistake visibility for velocity.

This has important implications for how we think about wealth itself. If money is the storage of value across time, then the ability to relate wisely to time is a precondition for meaningful wealth-building. Owners do not simply invest money—they invest time. They design feedback loops that compound not just interest, but insight. They are not seduced by immediacy because they understand that most meaningful gains are non-linear. Time, properly leveraged, produces effects far beyond what effort alone can generate.

This mindset is also visible in how people respond to volatility. Those operating from a short-term frame tend to panic, retreat, or overcorrect when disruptions occur. Owners, by contrast, expand their aperture. They understand that disruptions are part of any long-range endeavour. In fact, many of them expect to be misunderstood or criticised in the short term. Their orientation toward time gives them the psychological distance required to make unpopular, yet necessary, choices. This is not stoicism as posture—it is time intelligence as strategy.

It is not accidental that many of the world's most successful family businesses, such as S.C. Johnson or the Rothschild banking dynasty, build their governance structures to reinforce long-term thinking. They embed multi-generational vision into their operating models. Decisions are not made for one fiscal year, but for one or two lifetimes. This framing recalibrates what counts as "success" and what warrants "risk." When the timeframe is expanded, so is the willingness to delay gratification and absorb short-term discomfort.

But this kind of thinking is not limited to elite institutions or multi-million-pound portfolios. It is available to anyone willing to unlearn the default urgency of consumer culture. One of the most transformative exercises any individual can undertake is to stretch their mental time horizon. Imagine thinking not just about what you want by the end of the year, but what you would like to have made possible in twenty. Imagine asking not just what goals to set, but what foundations to pour—for your children, for your community, for your legacy.

Doing so changes everything. It alters what you pay attention to. It recalibrates your relationship to distraction. It strips the shine off short-term signalling games—likes, trends, quick wins—and re-centres what actually compounds: trust, skill, reputation, alignment. Most importantly, it allows for the type of decision-making that prioritises quality over optics and resilience over immediacy.

In practice, thinking in longer timeframes does not require predicting the future. It requires positioning for durability. Amazon's Jeff Bezos, famously indifferent to quarterly Wall Street expectations, described the company's strategic edge as its willingness to think on a seven-year horizon, while competitors optimised for two or three. His point was not that Amazon could see the future with greater clarity—it was that they could absorb the uncertainty of time better than most. That absorption capacity *is* the competitive advantage.

There is also an ethical component to temporal orientation. When we make decisions with longer timelines in mind, we are more likely to account for second-order consequences—on others, on systems, on future generations. This is why indigenous models of decision-making often reference "seven-generation thinking." The question is not merely what is profitable today, but what will be honourable, sustainable, and beneficial for descendants not yet born. This approach challenges the extractive logic of modern capitalism, asking us to be not only agents of wealth but trustees of time.

In individual terms, this might mean saying no to opportunities that promise rapid financial gain but misalign with values. It might mean investing in education, health, or skill development that does not yield immediate return but strengthens the foundation for decades to come. It might mean taking the harder path—building something original, mentoring someone deeply, restoring a relationship—because you understand that significance compounds more meaningfully than status.

To play the inner game of time is to engage in one of the rarest forms of agency available in modern life: the ability to choose duration over distraction. It is to detach from the default tempo of algorithms, content cycles, and commercial urgency, and instead reorient toward rhythm, intention, and legacy. It is to understand that the most powerful assets—trust, clarity, mastery, and time itself—are not bought or borrowed. They are built, slowly and deliberately, by those who choose to own their time instead of renting it out to every demand.

And that is the essence of ownership: the refusal to let time use you. The commitment to put it to work—not only for profit, but for purpose. Not only for survival, but for significance. The owner's mind does not merely optimise minutes. It stewards decades. And in doing so, it produces something rare in any market—durable wealth, quietly compounding, across lifetimes.

The Invisible Cost of a Consumer Mindset

At first glance, consumption appears harmless—even necessary. We buy what we need, what we want, and what we believe reflects who we are. The consumer economy is predicated on this cycle: earn, spend, repeat. Yet beneath the surface of modern consumption lies a cost structure few people see. Not just in pounds and pence, but in autonomy, emotional clarity, time allocation, and ultimately, long-term wealth. The consumer mindset is not merely a behavioural pattern; it is a lens through which meaning, status, and satisfaction are distorted. And it is quietly expensive—not only financially, but psychologically and existentially.

A consumer mindset is reactive by nature. It functions on a stimulus-response loop: we see, we want, we acquire. But the process doesn't end with acquisition; it resets. Consumption satisfies only briefly, which is precisely what sustains its economic viability. The system is designed not to fulfil, but to perpetuate. This is not a conspiracy—it is a commercial model that thrives on insatiability. The invisible cost is that over time, individuals internalise a worldview where value must be purchased and identity must be performed.

Reactive consumption is not confined to shopping or material goods. It seeps into how people approach life decisions. Job selection based on salary optics. Education pursued for credentialism rather than depth. Leisure optimised for display rather than rest. Social media, rather than simply reflecting behaviour, accelerates it—rendering consumption both visible and comparative. It is not enough to go on holiday; it must be shared. Not enough to buy the watch; it must signal something to someone else. The result is a slow erosion of internal metrics. Validation is outsourced. And in that outsourcing, meaning degrades.

The consumer mindset confuses wants with needs and aesthetic alignment with actual alignment. It treats money as a tool for identity management rather than freedom. The distinction matters deeply. When money is used to signal who you are—or who you hope others think you are—it becomes performative. When money is used to invest in capacities, relationships, or assets that increase agency, it becomes transformative. One reinforces dependency; the other builds autonomy.

This dynamic is not accidental. The architecture of modern economies depends on consumers making emotionally charged, short-sighted decisions. Delayed gratification is good for financial independence, but bad for quarterly revenue. The incentives are misaligned. And so marketing has evolved not simply to inform, but to shape identity. Products are no longer things; they are expressions of values, markers of aspiration, and tools for psychological self-regulation. Buying becomes a substitute for becoming.

Over time, this behaviour calcifies. The consumer's decision-making apparatus is wired for short-term optimisation. Time is spent rather than allocated. Energy is scattered across options rather than concentrated on priorities. Money is leaked through small indulgences that, taken individually, seem trivial—but in aggregate, steal the capital needed to make meaningful investments. This is what makes the consumer mindset so expensive. It erodes the conditions necessary for compounding—focus, patience, and clarity of intent.

Contrast this with the owner's mindset. Where the consumer reacts, the owner designs. The owner allocates resources—money, time, attention—with a view toward reinforcement. Purchases are not merely about utility or image; they are about alignment. Does this expenditure move me closer to who I'm becoming? Does it sustain or distract? The owner does not demonise consumption, but contextualises it. There is a place for pleasure, aesthetic appreciation, and enjoyment. But they are held within a broader framework. Spending is not morally wrong. It is strategically evaluated.

One of the most telling examples of this shift is seen in how individuals handle windfalls—unexpected income, bonuses, or inheritances. Those operating from a consumer mindset typically see windfalls as permission to consume: an upgraded car, a luxury holiday, a larger home. Those operating from an ownership mindset ask a different question: *What can this capital free me to do, build, or secure?* This is not about frugality. It is about intentionality. It is about refusing to convert every increase in resources into a proportionate increase in lifestyle overhead.

The long-term consequences are profound. Consumption-driven validation is volatile. It requires constant replenishment and is uniquely vulnerable to social comparison. As soon as a peer acquires more, the bar resets. Meaning, in this context, is fragile—tethered to external variables and trends. Investment-driven meaning, by contrast, is stabilised by alignment with deeply held values. It may be less visible, but it is vastly more durable. It allows a person to feel centred during market volatility, career transitions, or moments of public invisibility. It provides ballast.

The psychological toll of consumption is also cumulative. Each impulsive purchase may seem isolated, but it leaves a residue. Guilt, shame, rationalisation—all of these consume cognitive bandwidth. When spending becomes habitual, it creates noise that obscures actual priorities. Budgeting, then, becomes an exercise in managing chaos rather than expressing intention. Many people are not overextended financially because they have too little income; they are overextended because their spending patterns are reactive and misaligned. Ownership, in this sense, is about coherence.

There is also a deeper ethical dimension. A consumer orientation often externalises consequences—environmental, social, or relational. Fast fashion, for instance, offers the illusion of affordability while obscuring the exploitation embedded in its supply chain. Single-use convenience products deliver momentary satisfaction but contribute to long-term degradation. The owner, by contrast, considers second-order effects. They understand that every purchase is a proxy vote for a particular kind of world. Money is not neutral; it is directive.

From a developmental perspective, the consumer mindset is often inherited. Children learn by observation. If they see adults using money as a coping mechanism, a tool for status assertion, or a substitute for presence, they internalise these functions long before they grasp financial concepts. They associate spending with reward, emotional relief, or social elevation. Without intervention, these patterns are carried into adulthood—unquestioned, unexamined, and entrenched. The work of financial maturity, then, is not only economic—it is psychological and intergenerational.

One way to interrupt this cycle is through clarity of purpose. People who have a defined vision for their life—beyond consumption—spend differently. They are less vulnerable to manipulation because their attention is anchored. They are not immune to impulse, but they are more capable of contextualising it. Vision, in this sense, is a form of immunity. It filters noise. It lowers susceptibility to marketing that trades on fear, scarcity, or comparison. It enables what behavioural economists call *precommitment*: the ability to make decisions today that protect your future self from your present impulses.

This is why ownership is less about net worth and more about narrative. It is the story you tell yourself about what your life is for, and the role money plays within that story. The consumer story is episodic: it begins and ends with each transaction. The owner's story is longitudinal: each decision is a chapter in a broader arc. Consumption becomes occasional punctuation—not the plot itself.

There are practical implications for professionals and families alike. A professional earning six figures but outsourcing emotional regulation to spending will eventually feel unmoored. Their lifestyle will grow, but their sense of sovereignty will not. A family that teaches budgeting but not values-based spending will raise children who know how to track expenses but not how to allocate meaningfully. Ownership requires integration. It is not just a financial skillset; it is a worldview.

To escape the invisible cost of consumption, one must first see it. Not only on statements or spreadsheets, but in attention residue, emotional fatigue, and opportunity cost. What could have been built, invested, or contributed if consumption weren't reflexive? What margin—of time, of money, of peace—might have been created? These are not theoretical questions. They are diagnostic tools.

In the end, the cost of a consumer mindset is not primarily material. It is existential. It is the cost of living according to someone else's definition of success. It is the cost of outsourcing your sense of value to external inputs. It is the cost of forfeiting authorship of your own life in exchange for momentary validation.

Ownership offers a way out—not through austerity, but through authorship. It reclaims spending as a form of self-expression, not self-erasure. It transforms money from a means of escape to a medium of alignment. And that shift—from consumption to construction, from validation to vision—is where wealth truly begins.

Chapter 2
The Infinite Ledger

The conventional balance sheet measures what can be counted—assets, liabilities, cash flows. Yet it overlooks what truly sustains wealth across time: trust, reputation, relational depth, institutional memory, and the values that underpin decisions. These are not airy abstractions; they form the intangible scaffolding of enduring prosperity. This chapter introduces the concept of the infinite ledger—a multi-generational, multidimensional view of wealth that transcends personal lifespan and reframes success from mere accumulation to stewardship. It challenges the transactional mindset prevalent in modern finance and asks instead: what endures, and how do we cultivate it?

To think in terms of an infinite ledger is to leave behind the quarterly-report mentality and embrace the perspective of lineage. It demands a shift from immediacy to longevity, from extraction to cultivation. While most financial frameworks prioritise outputs, the infinite ledger emphasises throughput—what flows through us, whether resources, ideas, or values—and how we condition those flows for the benefit of others, often unseen. The question becomes not, "What can I gain?" but, "What can I nurture, and how will it persist beyond my lifetime?"

The chapter opens with the principle of generational thinking, not transactional thinking. This is not mere poetic flourish; it is a practical strategy employed by the world's most enduring family businesses, indigenous societies, and ecological systems. Consider the Haudenosaunee Confederacy's "Seventh Generation Principle," which instructs leaders to make decisions with the welfare of seven generations in the future in mind. This is not abstract futurism—it is a disciplined moral and strategic filter guiding present behaviour.

Family enterprises with multi-generational success—such as S.C. Johnson, stewarded by the same family for over 130 years—do more than preserve operational continuity. They deliberately transmit values. Rituals, shared language, and written family philosophies protect more than capital; they preserve clarity. Legacy, these families understand, is not a posthumous gift but a framework actively designed during life.

In practical terms, legacy becomes a continuous design process. The infinite ledger is written in real time through policies, conversations, decisions, and investments. Every choice, however granular, contributes to a broader timeline. Thinking this way reshapes priorities: status is traded for resilience, convenience for integrity, short-term return for durability. Questions emerge: Will this choice hold value in two decades? What precedent does it establish? Whose values are honoured? What norms are reinforced?

Living according to an infinite ledger demands a departure from scarcity thinking. Scarcity, though sometimes rooted in real limits, becomes pathological when it defines identity. It breeds short-termism, hoarding, and transactional relationships. Time feels urgent, others feel threatening, and generosity seems indulgent. Stewardship, by contrast, restores agency. It recognises limits without being paralysed by them, framing capital—financial, relational, intellectual—not as possession but as a resource to deploy with intention. The guiding question becomes: how can I grow this well, and for whom? Stewardship is both an ethic and an investment philosophy.

Take Patagonia, for example. The company transferred ownership into a trust designed to preserve its environmental mission indefinitely. Misread by some as eccentric philanthropy, the move was, in fact, a masterstroke of strategic stewardship: it rendered the company's capital engine regenerative, institutionalised mission, and ensured legacy. The infinite ledger, in action, is a decision whose impact exceeds the lifespan of its architects.

Yet the paradox of enough complicates matters, particularly for high-achievers. In cultures that glorify expansion, sufficiency is often mistaken for complacency. Implicit messages insist: if more is possible, it must be pursued. Blind pursuit of growth carries hidden costs: burnout, ethical compromise, distortion of intent. When "more" becomes automatic, clarity diminishes, and resources are diverted to maintaining momentum rather than refining purpose.

Ancient wisdom offers a corrective. Stoics like Seneca remind us that wealth lies not in vast possessions but in having few wants. Buddhist economics, articulated by thinkers such as E.F. Schumacher, frames prosperity not as consumption but as the harmony of means and ends. Neither perspective advocates passivity; both champion precision. Knowing what constitutes "enough" allows surplus to become stewardship, turning capital from a burden into a tool.

The paradox of enough is not minimalism for its own sake. It is an invitation to identify the point of diminishing returns—financially, psychologically, ethically. Once enough is clarified, priorities sharpen, pace moderates, and optionality increases. Focus becomes a function of intentional constraint.

Focus is the cornerstone of durability. In systems theory, durability is not rigidity. The most resilient systems incorporate variability without collapse. Nassim Taleb's concept of antifragility is instructive: fragile systems break under stress; robust systems endure; antifragile systems improve when challenged. An investor with an antifragile portfolio does not merely survive a downturn—they emerge stronger, having refined assumptions and seized opportunity.

This principle extends beyond finance to careers, families, and belief systems. The infinite ledger is inherently antifragile. It is grounded in principles—integrity, adaptability, clarity—that endure volatility. It prioritises systems over outcomes and liberates individuals from the trap of over-optimisation.

Engaging with this chapter means entering a ledger that cannot be quantified but governs what truly matters. You will be asked to consider not the immediate gain, but coherence across generations; not short-term profit, but long-term value and defendable principles. Frameworks for mapping legacy, case studies of companies and cultures operating on long-range logic, and tools for transitioning from scarcity to stewardship will guide this exploration.

This is demanding work. It requires abandoning cultural obsession with immediacy, cultivating patience, humility, and comfort with incomplete rewards. The payoff is profound: a financial philosophy rooted in integrity, continuity, and contribution. The infinite ledger does not promise speed; it promises meaning. And that promise is worth the effort it demands.

Thinking in Generations, Not Transactions

The shortest question in finance is also the most consequential: *What is your time horizon?* For most people, the answer is reflexive—twelve months, maybe five years, possibly retirement age. Rarely do individuals or institutions think beyond their own lifespans. But every enduring system—from ancient cultures to successful multigenerational businesses—operates on a much longer clock. Their strategic posture is not defined by quarters or campaigns, but by continuity. To think generationally is not merely to adopt a long-term mindset. It is to change the very grammar of decision-making—from what serves *me* now, to what serves *us* later. The difference is not in scale. It is in orientation. Transactional logic is extractive. Generational logic is regenerative.

The prevailing logic of modern markets favours speed, scale, and liquidity. It rewards the short-term optimiser, the hyper-efficient tactician, the operator who can move fast and exit faster. The consequence of this approach is visible everywhere: brittle companies built for valuation, not value; families fractured over inheritance rather than unified by shared stewardship; individuals caught in the churn of productivity without clarity of legacy. The metrics that dominate conventional success narratives—net worth, career milestones, portfolio performance—are often blind to whether anything truly enduring has been created. If you build something that doesn't outlive your involvement, can it really be called wealth?

Family businesses provide a counterpoint—sometimes flawed, but frequently instructive. The most enduring among them are structured not around individual ambition, but around continuity of purpose. Consider the Danish shipping company Maersk, founded in 1904, or Japanese conglomerates like Takenaka Corporation, which has operated under family leadership since the 1600s. These organisations are not accidents of longevity. They are the result of explicit design choices: reinvesting in people, favouring durable over fashionable growth, and embedding family governance frameworks that prioritise coherence over charisma. They understand that *succession is not an event; it is a culture.*

The difference lies in temporal framing. A founder thinking transactionally may ask, "How do we scale this quickly?" A generational thinker asks, "How do we preserve integrity through scale, and hand it off stronger than we found it?" These are not merely philosophical questions. They shape capital allocation, hiring practices, brand strategy, and even legal structures. The implications are especially acute when institutions face volatility. Businesses driven by short-term incentives tend to retrench. Those anchored by generational clarity lean into resilience. They act as if someone is always watching who hasn't yet been born.

Indigenous worldviews offer perhaps the most refined articulation of this perspective. Among many First Nations communities in North America, decisions are made in reference to the seventh generation—those who will be born long after current leaders have died. This principle is not symbolic. It is regulatory. It governs environmental policy, resource use, and communal structures. It creates a temporal accountability rarely seen in corporate or personal finance. To think in generations is to embed humility into governance. You are not the endpoint. You are a link in a long chain. And your responsibility is not to maximise, but to *transmit.*

Nature models this thinking at an even deeper level. Ecosystems regenerate through feedback loops that prioritise stability over speed. Forests do not clearcut themselves to increase quarterly yield. They develop over cycles of disturbance and renewal. Species adapt to balance, not conquest. The most resilient systems are biodiverse, interdependent, and responsive—not mechanistic, extractive, or hyper-optimised. When wealth systems ignore these principles, they become fragile. When they incorporate them—through diverse assets, redundancy, relational capital—they become antifragile.

Yet in personal finance, we rarely build on such terms. Individuals are taught to think in tactical intervals—saving for retirement, paying off a mortgage, hitting an income bracket. These are important, but they are structurally limited. They do not account for the longer arc of intergenerational transmission: how values are passed, how narratives are inherited, how institutions are built to outlast their architects. Without this frame, wealth becomes not a tool for continuity but a source of confusion and conflict.

Consider the difference between inheritance and legacy. Inheritance is the transfer of assets. Legacy is the transfer of intention. The former can be executed by lawyers; the latter requires lived commitment. A parent who leaves money but fails to cultivate financial literacy or emotional maturity in their children passes on not security but volatility. In contrast, a parent who models stewardship, invests in clarity of family purpose, and treats money as a shared tool for meaningful contribution leaves behind a *narrative structure*—one that can guide decisions long after the original capital is spent.

Mapping personal legacy timelines is a critical exercise for those seeking to move from transactional behaviour to generational thinking. This is not a vision board exercise. It is a form of strategic planning that includes not only what you wish to achieve in your lifetime, but what you hope will remain active beyond it. Start by identifying key inflection points: what foundational values were passed to you (explicitly or implicitly)? What decisions have compounded positively or negatively over time? What do you wish to remain legible to your descendants—not just in terms of assets, but in terms of decisions made and reasons given?

Then ask: What am I building that will still serve, matter, or speak when I am no longer here to explain it? What systems—financial, relational, intellectual—am I embedding with enough clarity that they can be maintained and evolved by others without my constant presence? What would it take for my absence to strengthen what I've created rather than diminish it?

These are not abstract questions. They are architectural. They lead to different behaviours. Someone who thinks transactionally might delay estate planning until their 60s. A generational thinker engages it in their 30s, not out of morbidity, but out of clarity. A transactional approach may focus on returns alone. A generational perspective considers *where* those returns are directed, *what* they empower, and *who* is positioned to carry them forward responsibly. This is not risk aversion; it is risk redefinition.

There is a tension, of course. Thinking generationally can feel at odds with the culture of immediacy. It requires the willingness to slow down, to forgo shortcuts, to invest in processes that may bear fruit only in decades. This is difficult, especially in high-performance environments that reward urgency over durability. But the rewards of generational thinking compound exponentially. They include reputational trust, relational cohesion, narrative clarity, and institutional longevity. These are not soft benefits. They are hard strategic advantages.

The mindset shift is subtle but profound. It involves moving from ownership of *things* to stewardship of *meaning*. It changes your orientation to risk, to time, to impact. And most importantly, it transforms your financial decisions from reactive moves on a spreadsheet to deliberate entries on a much longer ledger—one that tracks not only capital but contribution, not only valuation but values.

To think in generations is to play a longer game. But more than that, it is to recognise that you are already part of a game in motion—one whose origins precede you and whose outcomes will extend far beyond your control. The question is not whether you're part of a legacy. It is whether that legacy has been authored with intention or shaped by inertia. This chapter invites you to choose the former. Not simply to think bigger, but to think longer. And through that extension of time, to gain something the market will never offer: continuity with purpose.

From Scarcity to Stewardship

Most financial decisions are not made on spreadsheets. They are made in the quieter, less visible corridors of emotion—shaped not by data, but by belief. At the root of many decisions that stall, diminish, or sabotage wealth-building is a deeply ingrained orientation toward *scarcity*. Scarcity is not simply the absence of resources. It is the *assumption* of insufficiency. It distorts perception, narrows time horizons, and fosters reactive behaviour. Scarcity says: protect what you have. Stewardship says: grow what you're responsible for. The distinction between the two is subtle, but in practice, it changes everything—from how people invest their capital to how they lead organisations and allocate attention.

Scarcity thrives on the illusion of certainty. It clings tightly to what feels familiar, even if what is familiar is limiting. It generates risk aversion, defensiveness, and a preference for low-variance outcomes. Under scarcity thinking, preservation becomes a proxy for success. And while preservation has its place, it does not scale into purpose. Scarcity convinces individuals and institutions alike to aim for survival rather than resilience, stagnation rather than evolution. What makes this so dangerous is that it often masquerades as prudence. But beneath the surface, it is driven by fear—of loss, irrelevance, or exposure.

Stewardship offers a fundamentally different posture. It begins not with the fear of losing, but with the responsibility to multiply—not merely assets, but value in the broadest sense. Stewardship is not ownership alone. It is the *careful design of continuity*. A steward is not just a user of resources, but a curator of outcomes—for the future, for others, and often for successors they will never meet. This mindset shift has implications far beyond individual psychology. It reorients how capital is allocated, how companies are structured, and how legacy is transmitted.

The American outdoor clothing company Patagonia offers perhaps the most high-profile and instructive example. In 2022, founder Yvon Chouinard transferred ownership of the $3 billion business into a specially designed trust and non-profit. Rather than cashing out or listing the company, he ensured that all profits would be directed toward environmental causes in perpetuity. The structure was radical not because it was anti-capitalist, but because it was *post-scarcity*. Chouinard recognised that the company was never his to hoard or monetise. It was something he had helped build and had a duty to protect—not as an asset, but as a vehicle of meaning. This is stewardship in practice: the deliberate forfeiture of control in favour of continuity, aligned with values, and structured for perpetuation.

The key feature of stewardship is not self-denial, but systems thinking. Where scarcity sees discrete outcomes—quarterly earnings, isolated transactions—stewardship sees ecosystems. It asks how today's decision will reinforce or erode tomorrow's capacity. This is visible in the governance structure of S.C. Johnson, one of the world's most successful family-owned businesses. For over a century, the Johnson family has embedded stewardship into the company's DNA—not just through environmental initiatives, but through active succession planning, long-term reinvestment, and a refusal to dilute control for short-term gains. The result is a company that has weathered economic cycles, technological disruptions, and generational handovers with its identity and integrity intact.

Stewardship reframes investment itself. Under scarcity, investment is often seen as a gamble—something to be tightly monitored, nervously adjusted, and evaluated constantly. It is measured in short-term performance and benchmarked against peers. But stewardship treats investment as cultivation. The question is not *what can I extract,* but *what can I nurture, and at what pace will it grow best?* This applies equally to financial assets, professional relationships, intellectual capital, and family legacies. The steward allocates not for immediate gain, but for structural coherence. They do not simply ask if something will grow—they ask whether its growth will matter in ten, twenty, or fifty years.

This orientation also impacts how we think about wealth preservation. Traditional estate planning, for instance, is often governed by defensive architecture—mechanisms designed to avoid tax, protect from lawsuits, and lock in structures that limit future flexibility. While some of this is necessary, stewardship goes further. It asks: *What values are these structures preserving? What beliefs are we embedding in our children through these systems?* A trust that distributes wealth automatically without embedded expectations or education does not preserve legacy—it endangers it. A stewardship model, by contrast, includes governance, story, education, and rituals. It creates alignment between resources and responsibility. It makes the passing on of wealth not a transaction, but a handover of vision.

Critically, stewardship does not ignore risk. It embraces it—but redefines it. Scarcity sees risk as loss. Stewardship sees unmanaged potential as a risk. A steward understands that failing to act, failing to invest, or failing to prepare a successor carries its own costs. The risk is not just volatility—it is *fragility*. When fear dominates decision-making, people tend to over-index on protection and under-index on preparation. A scarcity mindset builds moats. A stewardship mindset builds bridges.

The transition from scarcity to stewardship also requires a reframing of metrics. What gets measured, after all, shapes behaviour. If performance is measured purely in financial returns, stewardship will always appear inefficient. It may prioritise sustainability over speed, culture over quarterly results, and intergenerational health over short-term dominance. But these "inefficiencies" are precisely what create long-term strength. Patagonia's choice to donate its profits may look irrational through a traditional finance lens—but from a stewardship perspective, it is an elegant form of capital deployment: risk-managed, purpose-aligned, and reputation-building.

This reframing applies equally to personal life. A professional who operates from scarcity may view career decisions through the lens of salary, title, or status. A steward considers coherence. Does this role align with my larger purpose? Does it position me to invest in others, not just extract value? Am I building something that can be sustained without my constant presence? The scarcity-driven worker optimises for control. The steward designs for succession.

One of the most powerful ways to operationalise stewardship is through policy—not governmental, but *personal.* Formalising intent into repeatable systems creates clarity and resilience. This can include legacy letters to heirs, investment mandates grounded in values, or family charters that define not only what assets exist but why they exist and how they should be stewarded. These tools are not performative. They are interpretive frameworks—designed to outlive the original decision-maker and ensure that meaning is preserved alongside money.

None of this is to suggest that scarcity is irrational. It is often inherited, reinforced by experience, and socially validated. Many first-generation wealth builders, in particular, carry scars from volatility and precarity. The instinct to protect is real. But at some point, protection must give way to design. Scarcity is a season. It cannot become a worldview. If it does, the very wealth it tries to preserve becomes brittle—structurally incapable of evolution, unable to adapt, unable to be handed on.

Stewardship, then, is not a soft ideal. It is a hard discipline. It requires patience, system thinking, and the willingness to measure success not just by what is gained, but by what is preserved, multiplied, and made meaningful. It requires letting go of control in order to build structures that do not require constant oversight. It requires trust—not in blind optimism, but in well-governed systems, aligned incentives, and clear principles.

The most effective stewards understand that they are not the culmination of anything. They are a *conduit*. Their role is not to dominate the system, but to prepare it for those who will come after. This is not an abdication of agency. It is its highest expression: agency not merely used for private gain, but for public, familial, or organisational continuity.

To move from scarcity to stewardship is not to become less rigorous—it is to become more responsible. It is to think in systems, act with intention, and orient decision-making toward outcomes that matter over decades, not weeks. It is to treat wealth not as a fortress to guard, but as a garden to cultivate—and ultimately, to pass on with care.

The Paradox of Enough

Most people never define what "enough" means. They chase it instinctively, vaguely, as if it were a moving target they might eventually stumble upon. This ambiguity is not benign—it is architecturally dangerous. Without a clear understanding of sufficiency, ambition becomes indistinguishable from anxiety. More becomes the default. And more, as countless high performers and high earners eventually discover, is not a strategy—it is an addiction. The paradox of enough lies in this: *only those who know what is sufficient can ever experience true abundance*. Without that clarity, wealth becomes noise and freedom becomes elusive.

The cultural context exacerbates the problem. Modern capitalist societies are built on perpetual dissatisfaction, not because of malicious intent, but because dissatisfaction is commercially productive. If everyone felt content, growth would slow. So we are taught—subtly, pervasively—that more is always better: more income, more visibility, more followers, more optionality. This bias permeates everything from career trajectories to investment decisions to how we measure self-worth. The result is a deeply ingrained assumption: *success means expansion.* But when expansion is untethered to meaning, it creates strategic blindness. Time, energy, and capital are scattered across pursuits that serve ego more than purpose.

This is where clarity around "enough" becomes not just a philosophical exercise but a form of cognitive and strategic liberation. It is the mental boundary that allows for intentional focus. Without it, every opportunity is a temptation, every risk is a threat, and every win is an invitation to escalate. With it, trade-offs become obvious, decisions become simpler, and presence becomes possible. Defining enough is not about resignation—it is about *precision.* It is the quiet but powerful act of choosing coherence over compulsion.

Stoic philosophy has long recognised this principle. In *Letters to Lucilius*, Seneca writes, "Being poor is not having too little, it is wanting more." The Stoics did not reject wealth; they rejected enslavement to it. They trained themselves to *desire less*, not out of asceticism, but out of sovereignty. For the Stoic, enough was not a limit—it was an intentional choice to design life around internal values rather than external metrics. This perspective offered psychological invincibility. If your sense of sufficiency is internally defined, no external shock—financial, reputational, or relational—can destabilise your identity.

Buddhist economics articulates a similar logic, though from a different cultural lineage. E.F. Schumacher's seminal work, *Small Is Beautiful*, introduced the idea that economics should not be measured by output alone but by harmony between means and ends. In this model, the optimal state is not maximum consumption, but balanced sufficiency—where material needs are met without compromising spiritual clarity or ecological integrity. Here, the concept of "right livelihood" replaces the conventional obsession with scale. The goal is not to acquire endlessly but to live congruently.

Modern finance rarely engages with this question in a serious way. Financial planning tools can project net worth, model retirement timelines, and simulate market returns, but they cannot answer the deeper questions: *How much is enough? Enough for what? And according to whom?* When these questions remain unexamined, financial goals become proxies for unresolved psychological needs. A seven-figure portfolio may represent safety, but it may also be a buffer against perceived inadequacy. A prestigious job title may signal achievement, but it may also conceal an identity built on external validation. Without internal alignment, even success becomes a form of avoidance.

To understand the power of "enough," consider its impact on focus. Focus is the ability to say no—not arbitrarily, but deliberately. It is a function of clarity. When enough is defined, every new opportunity can be evaluated not just by its upside, but by its relevance to what already matters. Resources are no longer stretched to meet shifting goals. They are concentrated on sustaining a meaningful equilibrium. For many high performers, this shift is revolutionary. It reveals that the ceiling of performance is not determined by effort alone, but by *discernment.* And discernment requires a reference point. That reference point is sufficiency.

This applies equally to investment. Investors who have defined enough do not chase returns out of compulsion. They do not allocate capital to impress, to soothe anxiety, or to compete. They invest in alignment with a known threshold. This creates behavioural stability, which—over time—outperforms almost any other edge. The most consistent investors are not those with superior insight, but those with emotional clarity. They know what they are solving for. And because of that, they are less likely to be seduced by performance fads, liquidity traps, or fear-driven selloffs.

We see this same logic in the structure of durable family offices. The most resilient families do not simply preserve wealth—they define what the wealth is *for.* Their investment strategies reflect clearly articulated visions: educational access, generational entrepreneurship, philanthropic impact. With these anchors in place, they can say no to high-return strategies that compromise their values or increase fragility. Clarity around enough enables long-termism because it disciplines desire. It separates sustainable ambition from compulsive expansion.

There is also a neurological benefit. Neuroscience confirms that our brains are not wired for perpetual satisfaction. The dopamine system rewards novelty, not stability. This is why material satisfaction is often short-lived. The brain adapts quickly to a new baseline and begins seeking the next hit. Without conscious intervention, this creates a hedonic treadmill—constant motion with no lasting gain. Defining enough disrupts this cycle. It introduces a counterbalance: the prefrontal commitment to meaning over impulse. It creates a psychological stop-loss against burnout, comparison, and escalating lifestyle creep.

Practically, defining enough requires specificity. It cannot be vague. It involves asking uncomfortable but clarifying questions: *What standard of living am I truly committed to? What future am I responsible for enabling? What am I willing to trade for peace of mind, and what am I not?* These are not one-time reflections. They must be revisited regularly as life stages evolve. A twenty-five-year-old single entrepreneur and a fifty-five-year-old parent with dependents will have different answers—but both benefit from asking. The danger is not in having too little. It is in never pausing to consider what *would* be enough, even if it were within reach.

There is a tension here worth naming. In cultures that idolise high performance, the idea of sufficiency can sound like complacency. But this is a fundamental misunderstanding. Defining enough is not the death of ambition—it is its maturation. It means ambition has been interrogated, harnessed, and directed. It is no longer free-floating or reactive. It is strategic. The entrepreneur who says, "This is the scale I want, because it serves my values, my health, and my family," is not thinking small. They are thinking precisely.

Without that precision, ambition can devour its creator. History is littered with individuals who gained everything except perspective—who climbed ladders only to realise they were leaning against the wrong wall. By contrast, those who define enough build from the inside out. They know where they are going and why. And because they know, they can adapt, simplify, and pivot without the identity crisis that haunts those who tie their self-worth to ever-expanding outcomes.

At a societal level, redefining enough may be one of the most radical financial acts. It resists consumerism, decentralises ego, and decentralises extraction-based economics. It opens space for generosity, for intergenerational thinking, and for ecological stewardship. When individuals define what is enough, they often find that they need less than they assumed—and have more to contribute than they realised.

The paradox is this: the clearer your sense of sufficiency, the more capacity you unlock. Time becomes less fragmented. Money becomes less entangled with ego. Relationships become less transactional. Focus returns. And with it, peace—not as a static endpoint, but as a dynamic foundation for deeper work, better thinking, and more meaningful contribution.

This is the true power of enough. Not constraint, but clarity. Not retreat, but relevance. Not smaller dreams, but sharper ones. It is a philosophical filter, a behavioural compass, and a strategic asset—hidden in plain sight, waiting to be defined.

Why Durability Beats Returns

A portfolio that performs brilliantly on paper is of little value if it cannot survive real-world volatility. A career path that promises high earnings is hollow if it cannot sustain health, integrity, or adaptability over time. We are conditioned to chase returns—high percentages, fast outcomes, big wins. But returns are only one part of the equation. Durability is the part we neglect at our peril. The central insight here is this: *long-term resilience beats short-term optimisation.* In finance, in work, in systems, and in life, it is the structures that can endure stress—not merely outperform in calm—that end up defining true success.

This idea finds rigorous articulation in the work of Nassim Nicholas Taleb, whose concept of *antifragility* offers one of the most practical lenses for understanding why durability matters more than surface-level results. Fragile systems break under stress. Robust systems resist stress. *Antifragile systems*, however, improve through stress. They benefit from disorder, shocks, and variability. Crucially, they are not optimised for efficiency—they are designed for longevity, adaptability, and optionality. The distinction matters because what often looks like high performance in the short run—whether in markets, business models, or personal achievements—can conceal profound structural fragility.

Consider the difference between a speculative investment that delivers 35% annual returns but is dependent on leverage, low volatility, and perfect timing, and a diversified, dividend-producing portfolio that yields 8% but can absorb downturns, unexpected expenses, or periods of illiquidity. The former looks better—until it doesn't. One market event, policy shift, or technological disruption can erase years of gains, leaving the investor not just poorer, but destabilised. The latter grows more slowly, but survives longer, and most importantly, preserves the investor's optionality—the freedom to respond, adjust, and reallocate without crisis.

This is not a call for conservatism. It is a call for *structural intelligence.* Taleb puts it starkly: fragility is found in things that have more to lose than to gain from volatility. Antifragile assets and systems, on the other hand, gain from randomness. They are not rigid fortresses—they are flexible organisms. The mistake most people make is assuming that optimisation—maximising every variable—leads to strength. But maximisation often leaves no margin. It removes buffers, exhausts optionality, and creates invisible dependencies. That's not strength. That's fragility masquerading as efficiency.

The same logic applies to careers. A professional profile built for peak performance in one environment—say, high-growth tech or short-cycle consulting—may look exceptional until the context shifts. If that individual has over-specialised, neglected network diversity, or underinvested in regenerative skills, they are exposed. Compare that to a professional who has consciously maintained cross-domain fluency, developed multiple income streams, or built relationships outside their immediate vertical. Their "returns" may have been slower, less dramatic, but their *durability* is far greater. They can weather disruption, pivot without panic, and recover without implosion.

This insight explains why so many top-tier performers experience burnout, reputational collapse, or identity crises mid-career. They optimised for returns without designing for stress. Their careers were engineered like high-frequency trading algorithms: brilliant in bull markets, brittle in real life. Durability, by contrast, is quiet. It does not always reward immediacy. But it builds what actually matters: continuity, adaptability, and the capacity to evolve without losing coherence.

Family businesses that survive multiple generations provide rich case studies of this principle. They do not necessarily post the highest annual growth rates. But they are structured to endure. Companies like S.C. Johnson or Hermès have institutionalised mechanisms to slow decision-making, preserve mission continuity, and limit exposure to market whims. They often underperform their public competitors during bubbles—but they also do not implode when those bubbles burst. Their returns compound not because they are aggressive, but because they are *durable.* And durability, over time, *is* a form of return.

This perspective reframes how we think about risk. Traditional finance teaches that risk is the price of higher return. But this is a partial view. The better question is: *what kind of risk?* Risk that is visible, measured, and distributed wisely can be productive. Risk that is hidden, concentrated, or correlated with ego is dangerous. Fragile systems often underestimate the latter and overstate their control. Durable systems model humility—they expect to be wrong, build in buffers, and diversify not just across assets but across assumptions.

Optionality is central to this resilience. Taleb defines it as the ability to take advantage of favourable outcomes without requiring prediction. Antifragile systems are rich in optionality—they maintain flexibility, preserve liquidity, and decentralise decision-making. In financial terms, this may mean avoiding overly complex products or single-point failures. In career terms, it might mean preserving autonomy, staying psychologically mobile, or holding a cash cushion that allows you to walk away from misaligned roles.

Ironically, many high-return strategies destroy optionality. They lock people into golden handcuffs, force dependency on a single employer or industry, or require performance at unsustainable levels. The person making £500,000 a year may, in fact, have *less freedom* than the one making £120,000 with control over time, location, and project selection. When fragility is hidden behind prestige, optionality becomes the more accurate measure of wealth.

This lens also helps decode why some people thrive after failure while others are permanently set back. It is not necessarily a function of grit or willpower. Often, it is about system design. The durable thinker has accounted for failure—not emotionally, but structurally. They have left space for errors. They have redundancy in their systems, contingencies in their plans, and relationships built on more than performance. Fragile achievers, by contrast, live on a razor's edge—any disruption becomes existential.

The pursuit of durability does not preclude ambition. It channels it. It asks: *What can I build that not only succeeds, but survives me? What can I design that doesn't just outperform, but outlast?* These are not conservative questions. They are strategic ones. In fact, the most daring builders—entrepreneurs, artists, stewards of legacy—understand this intuitively. They make peace with slower growth in exchange for greater freedom. They play longer games.

And in long games, volatility is not an aberration. It is the environment. Those who prepare to thrive only in ideal conditions cannot endure. Those who design for variation, failure, and time—those who prioritise resilience over performance—outlast everyone.

This is why durability beats returns. Not because returns don't matter, but because *they only matter if you're still in the game*. Durability is what keeps you in the game. It allows you to recover, to adapt, to continue. It is not the opposite of growth. It is what enables it.

For individuals, families, and institutions aiming to build wealth with meaning, the question is not *what return can I get this year?* but *what system can I build that will still be delivering value—economic, personal, ethical—decades from now, even in my absence?* That system will not be the most optimised. It will be the most *alive*—capable of learning, absorbing shocks, and allocating attention where it matters most.

The future belongs not to the most aggressive, but to the most durable. And the wisest among us are already building accordingly.

Chapter 3
The Psychology of Capital

Money may be quantified in digits, but it is governed by emotion. On paper, it seems to obey logic, yet more often it bends to deep-seated beliefs, unconscious narratives, and impulsive reflexes. Traditional finance assumes rational actors—calculating risk, weighing opportunity costs, optimising returns. In reality, decisions around money are far less mechanical. They are shaped by scripts inherited from upbringing, cultural expectations, and emotional blind spots. Capital, in this sense, functions as a mirror. It reflects not only opportunity but also our fears, assumptions, and the identities we carry. Often, the clearest insight comes not from watching markets, but from observing what those markets reveal about ourselves.

This chapter delves beneath the numbers to explore the psychology of capital. It shifts focus from external tools—asset classes, portfolio theory, tax strategies—toward the internal architecture that quietly governs financial behaviour. Previous chapters examined time and legacy; here, we turn inward, dissecting the cognitive and emotional patterns that drive, distort, or deepen one's financial reality. The goal is not to psychologise for its own sake, but to build alignment between inner life and external financial actions.

Central to this exploration are money scripts and mental models: the hidden narratives operating beneath conscious awareness yet shaping choices consistently. Often, these scripts are inherited rather than taught. A child witnessing repeated parental arguments over spending may internalise money as conflict or danger. Another, raised amidst silent wealth, might learn that money is taboo—or a source of shame. Some, shaped by generational trauma, perceive money as power, survival, or moral leverage. These beliefs persist into adulthood, manifesting as spending patterns, investment biases, and distorted risk perceptions. Awareness of these scripts is not merely therapeutic; it is strategic. Even the most intelligent investor can sabotage outcomes if their internal narrative is dominated by scarcity, guilt, or compensatory behaviours.

Financial psychology increasingly employs structured prompts to surface these narratives: What did money signify in your childhood? When does financial anxiety surface, and why? Which purchases have carried shame, and which investments felt most meaningful? These are diagnostic tools, revealing the emotional infrastructure beneath apparently rational decisions. They expose where beliefs require updating, where behaviours are reactive rather than intentional, and where opportunity is unconsciously avoided because it conflicts with identity.

A fragile coupling often emerges between net worth and self-worth. In many professional spheres, financial success becomes synonymous with personal adequacy, creating an unstable sense of self, hypersensitive to fluctuations in income, valuation, or perception. Setbacks can trigger existential panic; successes may feel hollow, interpreted through a lens of inadequacy or comparison. Decoupling net worth from self-worth does not reject ambition or material success; it protects identity from volatility. Healthy metrics—integrity of decisions, alignment with values, long-term contribution—provide ballast in instability and clarity in abundance. They allow one to reject lucrative but misaligned opportunities, no longer driven by the need for external validation.

Such internal clarity proves invaluable in periods of uncertainty: market volatility, sudden loss, or economic disruption. These moments test not only strategy but emotional liquidity—the capacity to metabolise risk without reactivity. Composure is rarely innate; it is cultivated. Founders who lead through downturns, investors who hold conviction amid turbulence, individuals who pause rather than panic—these are not feats of stoicism, but reflections of internal regulation developed consciously and stress-tested over time.

Emotional liquidity does not suppress feeling; it creates space between stimulus and response. It enables observation of panic, scarcity narratives, and the urge to overcorrect, choosing instead to remain aligned with strategy. This capacity explains why some investors rebalance calmly while others sell in fear, and why certain leaders make unpopular decisions without internal collapse. Emotional liquidity is a hidden asset class underpinning effective long-term strategy, and unlike market returns, it can be directly cultivated—through reflection, coaching, somatic awareness, and adaptive planning.

Yet the subtlest threats are often daily, invisible: shame, envy, and avoidance. Shame encourages concealment of mistakes, compounding harm; envy distorts decisions, prompting imitation rather than alignment; avoidance masquerades as caution or busyness, delaying necessary action. These forces permeate all income levels, silently directing behaviour.

Addressing them demands cultural intelligence. Financial shame may stem from debt in one context, inherited wealth in another. Envy may arise from status in one scenario, from a desire for autonomy in another. Naming these emotions without moral judgement allows navigation with increasing choice, boundaries, and grace. Emotions are not obstacles—they are terrain.

This chapter guides readers through that terrain. It is not an instruction manual in emotional mastery, but a framework for understanding how capital interacts with identity, behaviour, and belief. Readers encounter case studies of individuals who reshaped lifelong money patterns through reflection, founders who built resilient business models by recognising bias, and exercises translating insight into action. It challenges assumptions about success, security, and what constitutes a meaningful financial life.

Ultimately, the psychology of capital is not about becoming emotionless. It is about emotional fluency: interpreting, integrating, and working with feeling rather than against it. It is designing a financial life that is not only technically sound but psychologically sustainable. Most financial failure does not stem from ignorance but from unexamined belief, reactive emotion, and misaligned identity. Enduring financial success arises when action aligns with authentic selfhood.

This chapter equips readers to cultivate that alignment: not to transcend emotion, but to integrate it; not to be immune to volatility, but to navigate it with composure; not to perform wealth, but to relate to it with clarity, stability, and quiet power. The true psychology of capital begins not in the market, but in the mirror.

Money Scripts and Mental Models

Most people believe they make financial decisions rationally—analysing data, comparing options, assessing risk. But beneath that surface, almost every choice involving money is filtered through internal narratives so ingrained we rarely question them. These subconscious patterns, known in financial psychology as *money scripts*, silently guide behaviour. They are not conscious strategies. They are inherited, emotional, and often outdated. Without scrutiny, they become mental ruts—biases masquerading as wisdom—that shape not only how we spend or save, but how we perceive value, define success, and relate to ourselves and others.

Money scripts are typically formed in childhood, through observation and experience, not instruction. A child who witnesses scarcity—whether through economic hardship or emotional deprivation—may develop an enduring fear of loss, even in abundance. Another raised in affluence but with inconsistent emotional connection might internalise the belief that wealth equates to love or attention. Some scripts are culturally reinforced: "You must work hard for money"; "Rich people are greedy"; "Money will solve everything." These ideas are absorbed without analysis, because they are absorbed before critical faculties are fully developed. They then operate as default settings, activated every time a decision involving money is made under stress, uncertainty, or pressure.

Mental models, by contrast, are the cognitive frameworks we consciously or unconsciously use to interpret financial situations. These might include principles like compounding, opportunity cost, or diversification. But even these frameworks are filtered through our scripts. A person who intellectually understands the value of long-term investing may still panic-sell in a downturn if their deeper money script is driven by scarcity or control. Conversely, someone with a high risk tolerance on paper may avoid growth investments altogether if they carry an unconscious belief that wealth invites conflict or moral compromise.

The challenge is that money scripts and mental models often operate in tension. Our intellect says one thing; our emotional memory insists on another. This is why personal finance advice, even when technically sound, fails to stick for so many people. It speaks to the rational mind while bypassing the narrative mind—the part that has been conditioned, shaped, and scarred by lived experience. To build financial systems that actually work, we must examine the stories underneath them.

Financial therapy offers a growing body of research-backed practices to uncover and revise these stories. One powerful method involves reflective inquiry—structured questions that reveal patterns through honest introspection. Consider the following prompts, not as exercises in abstraction, but as diagnostic tools:

What was the earliest memory you have of money, and how did it make you feel?

How did your caregivers talk about money—or avoid talking about it?

When you feel financially anxious, what do you fear will happen?

What beliefs about money have consistently guided your decisions, even when they didn't serve you?

When you experience financial success, what emotions surface—pride, guilt, fear, detachment?

Such questions are deceptively simple. But when answered with candour, they illuminate the emotional architecture beneath financial behaviour. They explain why someone with a six-figure income still feels unsafe, or why a financially secure individual resists investing, or why another compulsively gives away money they cannot afford to part with. These are not problems of arithmetic. They are issues of identity and belief.

The complexity increases when we realise these scripts do not exist in a vacuum. They are embedded within family systems, cultural narratives, and social conditioning. An individual from a family that valorised self-sacrifice may unconsciously resist building personal wealth, associating it with selfishness or betrayal. Another from a lineage of entrepreneurial trauma—bankruptcy, sudden loss, betrayal—may carry a quiet but powerful script that risk is shameful, or that success is fragile and must be hoarded. These beliefs do not make themselves known overtly. They surface in hesitation, overcomplication, avoidance, or sabotage.

Even mental models that are touted as objective can be misleading if they ignore context. Take the model of delayed gratification, often cited as a hallmark of financial maturity. While it can indeed support long-term planning, it may also reinforce scripts of deprivation for those raised in scarcity. Telling someone with deep economic trauma to "just delay gratification" can trigger defensive reactions or paralysis. For them, spending now is not irrational—it's an act of reclaiming agency. This doesn't mean all financial advice must be abandoned. It means advice must be integrated with self-awareness. *No model works if it collides with the underlying script that drives the person using it.*

Mental models become more reliable when they are calibrated with psychological insight. For instance, consider the model of "enough." When clearly defined, it can act as a stabilising anchor. But without clarity, the idea of "enough" becomes a moving target, distorted by comparison, media, and unresolved personal scripts. A person operating from a scarcity script may never feel enough, regardless of actual wealth. Their mental model of success will always reset just beyond reach. Conversely, someone who has interrogated their script may reach a powerful, grounded clarity on sufficiency—not as an act of resignation, but as a source of liberation. That shift is not financial—it is psychological. And it changes everything.

The practical application here is not to eliminate all scripts. That's neither realistic nor necessary. The goal is to *make them visible*, so they can be updated. Just as outdated software slows a system, outdated money scripts limit decision-making. When exposed, some scripts can be rewritten. Others can be reframed. Some can be retained but used with discernment. The process is not about perfection. It is about coherence—aligning financial decisions with conscious values, rather than unconscious fears.

To move in this direction, consider developing a *financial narrative audit.* Begin with past patterns. Where have you consistently underperformed your potential, and what emotion preceded that decision? Where have you overreached, and what were you trying to prove or compensate for? Next, examine your present strategies. Which ones feel life-giving, and which feel performative or driven by fear? Finally, look forward. What story do you want your financial life to tell, and what scripts must be confronted or updated to make that story possible?

This is not a soft exercise. It is foundational strategy. Investors who master this terrain often outperform not because they have better data, but because they have fewer internal contradictions. They are not triggered by market volatility in the same way. They are not chasing validation or avoiding discomfort. They can sit with uncertainty without collapsing into impulsivity or paralysis. That is not emotional luck. It is clarity earned through honest inquiry.

Understanding money scripts also enhances interpersonal dynamics. Many conflicts between partners, families, or teams around money are not about the numbers. They are about *mismatched scripts*. One person views saving as safety; another experiences it as deprivation. One sees spending as generosity; another sees it as recklessness. Without a shared awareness of these differing narratives, even the best-designed financial plans will strain under misunderstanding. With awareness, however, those tensions can become sites of growth—opportunities to design new models that honour multiple truths and move toward shared meaning.

In high-stakes environments—founding a company, leading an investment firm, stewarding intergenerational wealth—this work becomes even more essential. Leaders who are unaware of their own scripts project them onto systems. Scarcity becomes micromanagement. Guilt becomes over-accommodation. Control becomes rigidity disguised as prudence. But leaders who have examined their own narratives become far more effective at building teams, structuring capital, and making decisions that reflect not just their goals, but their wisdom.

The core message is this: *Financial intelligence without psychological insight is incomplete.* Knowing the market without knowing oneself is a recipe for chronic misalignment. But when self-awareness and strategy intersect, behaviour becomes coherent, risk becomes calibrated, and success becomes sustainable. This is not simply a better way to manage money. It is a more conscious way to relate to reality.

The reader willing to engage this work will find that the most impactful change often comes not from adding new tools, but from retiring old scripts. Financial clarity, it turns out, is not about knowing more. It is about seeing more—clearly, honestly, and with the courage to change what no longer serves. Once that happens, strategy becomes not just effective, but elegant. Because it is built on truth. And truth compounds better than any asset.

Emotional Liquidity: Handling Risk with Grace

Risk is not simply a matter of numbers. Volatility may be measured in percentage points and drawdowns, but the experience of risk is profoundly emotional. What determines whether a person panics, freezes, or responds strategically in uncertain times is not their access to data but their internal state—their *emotional liquidity*. Just as financial liquidity refers to how quickly assets can be converted into usable capital without significant loss, emotional liquidity describes a person's ability to stay responsive and grounded in the face of uncertainty without becoming emotionally insolvent.

The markets do not reward the smartest minds so much as the calmest hands. Investors and founders who build lasting wealth and institutional trust are not those who avoid risk, but those who develop the capacity to carry it *without collapsing into reactivity*. Emotional liquidity is not about suppressing emotion; it's about learning how to metabolise fear, uncertainty, and ambiguity in ways that keep decision-making clear, values-aligned, and antifragile over time.

One of the most misunderstood aspects of long-term investing and entrepreneurial leadership is how much of it is psychological endurance. The assumption that logic governs financial success is, at best, partial. Humans are not spreadsheets. When faced with the unknown, the primitive brain tends to default to the familiar scripts of fight, flight, or freeze. The challenge is not whether risk exists—

risk is constant—but whether we are capable of interpreting and responding to it with coherence and grace. This is where emotional liquidity becomes the most underappreciated asset in any financial or strategic portfolio.

Consider how seasoned investors like Howard Marks or Warren Buffett navigate downturns. They are not immune to fear, but they do not allow fear to hijack their process. Buffett's oft-quoted dictum, "Be fearful when others are greedy, and greedy when others are fearful," is not just market advice—it is a reflection of psychological discipline. It's an endorsement of *inverse emotional alignment*, the capacity to remain stable when others are destabilised. That trait is not innate; it is cultivated. And it depends on a set of practices that allow an individual to regulate emotional reactivity rather than outsource their sense of security to external conditions.

In the startup world, emotional liquidity is equally vital. Founders who cannot self-regulate tend to swing between grandiosity and despair—making reckless hires when flush, and brutal cuts when spooked. By contrast, those who build durable cultures and sustainable enterprises often carry what Jim Collins calls "productive paranoia"—a blend of cautious realism and calm preparation. They are not optimists in the blind sense, nor pessimists paralysed by possibility. They are grounded in emotional reality, able to metabolise stress without turning it into distortion.

Regulating emotion under stress is not a matter of willpower but of structure. One of the most effective tools for developing emotional liquidity is the *pause*. The deliberate act of not reacting immediately—to market drops, to a provocative email, to a fear of missing out—is in itself a discipline of power. The pause creates space for alignment: What am I feeling? What am I assuming? What do I actually know? What decision honours both logic and principle? In high-stakes environments, this split-second self-check can be the difference between irreversible mistakes and resilient positioning.

There is a psychological cost to poor liquidity that mirrors financial illiquidity. When we are emotionally over-leveraged—invested in outcomes we cannot control, dependent on short-term signals for validation—we become vulnerable to every fluctuation. We cannot think long-term because we are psychologically margin-called by the moment. Every drop feels existential. Every delay feels unbearable. This is how people burn out, sell low, overextend, or abandon well-considered plans. Their emotions, not the market, have liquidated their future.

But emotional liquidity also has positive compounding effects. The investor who can sit through noise is more likely to realise gains that others forfeit. The founder who can resist premature scaling or avoid reactive firing during a downturn builds credibility and cohesion. The board member who can hold tension without rushing to premature decisions contributes to a culture of considered governance. These advantages are not random. They are expressions of internal capital: calm, clarity, conviction.

At a deeper level, emotional liquidity is about how much psychological ambiguity one can tolerate without defaulting to control or collapse. The more an individual insists on certainty, the more brittle their strategies become. This is especially visible in personal investing. Many retail investors, for example, crave predictability and simplicity—"Just tell me where to put my money"—but this craving is often a response to emotional scarcity, not a lack of information. They want safety, not guidance. And this desire, when unchecked, leads them to over-concentrate, under-diversify, or chase charismatic but unstable financial advice.

True risk tolerance is not a checkbox on a brokerage form. It's a reflection of one's relationship to uncertainty, identity, and time. Someone who has built their self-worth entirely on performance metrics will find it excruciating to endure underperformance. Someone who has experienced economic trauma may interpret any setback as confirmation of doom. Emotional liquidity, then, must include the *ability to distinguish between the external event and the internal meaning we attach to it.* This is not self-help. It's strategic hygiene.

A useful exercise for enhancing emotional liquidity is to create a *risk response map.* Begin by identifying recent decisions made under pressure. Note what emotions arose—fear, shame, anger, urgency. Then trace what actions followed. Was there a deviation from plan? Was there an overcorrection or a delay? Finally, ask: What belief was driving that emotional response? Was it "I must not fail," or "This always happens to me," or "There won't be another chance"? These beliefs often lie at the root of poor risk handling—not the volatility itself.

Founders and investors who handle risk with grace often structure their environments to reduce reactivity. They build buffers: liquidity cushions, staggered hiring, adaptive timelines. But they also tend to cultivate environments where honest emotion is allowed without dominating. They have advisors who challenge their blind spots. They build rituals that promote perspective—walks, journaling, meditation, unplugging from news cycles. These practices are not luxuries. They are investments in the ability to see clearly when clarity is scarce.

Importantly, grace under risk does not mean detachment or passivity. It means *engaged neutrality*—a state in which one is deeply committed to purpose but not enslaved by outcome. This distinction is visible in investors like Ray Dalio, who uses systematic reflection and feedback to remain emotionally grounded, even amid significant losses. It's present in leaders like Yvon Chouinard, who built Patagonia not by maximising every financial return but by sustaining values under pressure—even when doing so incurred reputational and financial cost.

The capacity to absorb ambiguity without reaction, to feel fear without becoming fear-driven, to sense opportunity without becoming opportunistic—that is the mark of emotional liquidity. And like financial reserves, it must be cultivated when times are good, because its true value is revealed when conditions deteriorate.

This subchapter is not an appeal to stoicism for stoicism's sake. It is a call to emotional agility as a core component of financial and strategic mastery. Markets will convulse. Clients will change their minds. Governments will revise policies. Trends will reverse. What remains is the internal infrastructure: your capacity to regulate, reflect, and recalibrate.

That capacity—emotional liquidity—is not simply a trait. It is an advantage. And for those who cultivate it with seriousness, it becomes the margin of safety that no balance sheet can show but every outcome ultimately reflects.

Self-Worth and Net Worth: Decoupling the Two

In a culture where income is often confused with intelligence and wealth is mistaken for wisdom, few distortions are more persistent—or more personally corrosive—than the idea that financial outcomes reflect personal value. The entanglement of self-worth with net worth isn't merely a conceptual error. It quietly distorts behaviour, undermines resilience, and infects decision-making with shame, envy, or inflated pride. If left unexamined, it becomes a hidden operating system that ties a person's internal compass to external volatility, rendering both wealth creation and well-being hostage to market conditions and social comparisons.

At its core, this conflation stems from a misunderstanding of value. In markets, value is fluid, contextual, and transactional. A stock is worth what someone is willing to pay for it today. That does not make the company behind it either virtuous or vile—it makes it priced. But in human psychology, value has a deeper register. It's about dignity, agency, and contribution. When we allow the market's language to define the worth of a person, we're not just misusing economics; we're shrinking identity to a metric that was never meant to carry moral weight.

This is not just a philosophical concern. It has real-world implications. When people internalise the belief that higher net worth equates to higher self-worth, they often chase financial success for reasons that are fundamentally about validation rather than alignment. This leads to overwork, underrest, unnecessary risk-taking, or avoidance of necessary transitions—all in service of protecting an image rather than pursuing meaningful goals. Conversely, when financial setbacks occur—as they inevitably do in any long life—the shame can be paralyzing. People hesitate to seek help, avoid opportunities, or spiral into unproductive loops of self-judgement, because failure is no longer about a misstep; it's interpreted as a personal flaw.

Consider the stark difference between someone who sees money as a tool and someone who sees it as a scoreboard. The former can navigate fluctuations with detachment and strategic clarity. The latter is entangled. Every pay cut becomes an existential crisis. Every boom inflates ego rather than opportunity. Their financial decisions, whether aggressive or avoidant, are emotionally loaded. In financial therapy, such patterns are often traced to early experiences: the way a family talked—or didn't talk—about money, the emotional climate around spending, saving, or earning, and the silent stories that got encoded before reasoning ever had a chance to intervene.

The goal, then, is not to be indifferent to money but to *disentangle identity from financial performance.* This is not a call to spiritualise poverty or demonise success. It is an invitation to clarity. Net worth is a number. It is dynamic, external, and shaped by variables both within and beyond our control. Self-worth, by contrast, is a relationship—to oneself, one's values, and one's perceived capacity to contribute meaningfully. When the two become conflated, the person is effectively handing over their sense of self to a set of shifting valuations.

One powerful practice for decoupling these concepts is to articulate internal metrics for success. Instead of asking, "Am I earning enough?" or "Am I keeping up?", ask: *Did I act in integrity with what matters most to me today? Did I make decisions that align with my long-term vision? Did I move closer to the kind of life I consider meaningful?* These are not soft questions. They are structurally transformative. Over time, they train the mind to focus less on external validation and more on internal congruence. The paradox is that those who orient around internal metrics often make better financial decisions because they're less reactive, more patient, and more principled under pressure.

The corporate world offers countless examples of people whose net worth has soared while their inner life eroded—burned-out executives, overstretched founders, or high earners who remain emotionally bankrupt. Conversely, there are individuals—often less visible—who have lived with modest financial means but rich lives: secure in their identity, generous in their outlook, and aligned in their decisions. The difference is rarely intelligence or ambition. It is *emotional posture.* A person who views their finances as an expression of stewardship rather than self-definition can engage with risk, opportunity, and even loss with more grace and creativity.

Take, for example, a founder whose company fails after a decade of hard work. If their identity is enmeshed with the company's valuation, the collapse feels like personal annihilation. But if their identity is rooted in values—say, resilience, vision, or integrity—the failure is painful, but not definitive. They retain the psychological mobility to pivot, learn, and try again. Their self-worth provides ballast, not drag.

This is equally important in personal finance. A parent who ties their worth to earning capacity may miss years of relational presence chasing marginal gains. A professional who equates salary with status might ignore burnout signals or reject more meaningful but lower-paying opportunities. A retiree who has always measured success by accumulation may find themselves disoriented without a growing portfolio, even if they are financially secure. In each case, the problem is not money—it's misalignment between values and valuation.

To move toward decoupling, it is essential to surface the underlying scripts that drive the attachment. These often sound like: "I am only as good as my results." "If I don't earn more, I'm falling behind." "Success means being ahead of others." These scripts are rarely examined directly, yet they shape behaviour profoundly. Naming them is the first act of sovereignty. Once made visible, they can be interrogated, rewritten, or replaced with beliefs that are more sustainable and humane: "My value does not fluctuate with my income." "I can choose how I define enough." "What matters most is alignment, not applause."

An effective exercise is to draw two columns: in one, list the financial outcomes you desire—more savings, increased income, debt repayment, etc. In the other, list the qualities of personhood you want to embody—calm, clarity, discipline, generosity, freedom. Ask yourself which list currently determines your mood, your self-talk, and your decisions. Then ask which one *should*. This simple reflection can unmask the hidden levers of motivation and begin the work of building an identity that is no longer beholden to the market's mood swings.

Philosophical traditions have long understood the danger of tying self to externals. The Stoics, for instance, counselled that one's worth must reside in what is *within our control*: our choices, our character, our response to events. The Buddhists warned against attachment to transient forms, not because they denied the material world, but because they recognised the suffering that results from trying to extract permanence from impermanence. These are not merely spiritual maxims; they are blueprints for psychological durability in the face of an economy that will always fluctuate.

Decoupling self-worth from net worth does not mean ignoring money. It means relating to money from a centre of clarity rather than compulsion. It means defining wealth not merely as accumulation, but as the ability to live in alignment with what matters, even when doing so requires trade-offs. It means recognising that being rich in purpose, relationships, time, or trust is not inferior to being rich in assets—it is often more enduring.

Ultimately, the measure of a life well-lived is not its balance sheet but its coherence. When your internal sense of worth is intact, you are free to pursue, manage, and even lose money without losing yourself. That freedom is not just emotional. It is strategic. It allows for risk without recklessness, ambition without anxiety, and success without self-deception. It is the foundation upon which truly sustainable wealth—financial and otherwise—is built.

Shame, Envy, and the Hidden Drivers of Financial Behaviour

The most powerful forces in finance are not always visible in spreadsheets or markets—they reside in silence, in secrecy, and in stories we don't realise we are living out. For all the talk of compound interest and diversified portfolios, much of our behaviour with money is shaped by emotions we neither name nor fully understand. Among these, *shame* and *envy* are particularly potent. Quiet and corrosive, they operate beneath our conscious decision-making, distorting logic, driving compulsive action, and camouflaging themselves as ambition, prudence, or even morality. If we are to become true owners of our financial lives, these emotional drivers must be surfaced, understood, and integrated—not avoided or suppressed.

Shame and envy are not random afflictions. They are adaptive, if maladaptive, responses to a social environment that often equates financial status with human worth. Shame whispers: *You are behind.* Envy declares: *They are ahead.* These are not abstract sentiments. They manifest in behavioural patterns: chronic underspending or compulsive overconsumption; risk-aversion masquerading as responsibility; or overleveraging disguised as boldness. Behind the numbers, behind the trades, behind the budgets, lie stories about who we are, what we deserve, and how we compare.

To understand shame in the context of money, consider its origin: a sense of being fundamentally deficient in the eyes of others. Financial shame often begins early. A child growing up in a household where money was scarce or mismanaged may come to believe that financial failure is personal failure. They may internalise the belief that wealth is proof of competence and poverty is proof of character flaw. These narratives become hardwired and continue to shape adult financial choices, even if circumstances have changed. Someone may avoid looking at their bank account not out of laziness, but because it triggers a deep sense of inadequacy. Another may overwork not purely for income, but to outrun a private sense of unworthiness.

Envy, though more outwardly directed, is no less damaging. It emerges when we perceive someone else's financial situation as a threat to our own sense of adequacy. Envy is not mere desire—it's desire laced with self-negation. "I want what they have, and my lack of it makes me less." In a digital age, this emotion is constantly fuelled by curated displays of lifestyle and affluence. The result is a kind of low-grade existential dissonance. Even those with ample resources can feel poor—not because they lack, but because comparison creates artificial scarcity. Financial decisions made under the influence of envy are rarely sound. They tend to be reactive, performative, and untethered from personal values or strategic goals.

Case studies across wealth brackets confirm this. A middle-income professional might take on an unnecessary car lease to match perceived peer status. A high-net-worth individual might pursue a risky venture not for alignment, but because another investor in their circle posted a public win. The outcome isn't always ruinous, but the motivation is often unconscious. The issue is not intelligence or intention—it's misattributed desire. Without reflection, we confuse what is culturally rewarded with what is personally right.

One of the more insidious effects of these emotions is how they interact with identity. Shame can cause a person to believe they are "bad with money" and then unconsciously fulfil that prophecy through avoidance, self-sabotage, or inconsistent behaviour. Envy can lead someone to pursue wealth not for its utility or meaning, but to silence a feeling of inferiority. In both cases, money becomes not a means, but a mirror—one that reflects distorted images shaped by unresolved emotional patterns and societal conditioning.

Financial therapy and behavioural economics increasingly recognise these hidden drivers. In therapeutic settings, people often discover that a compulsive saver is not prudent, but anxious; a spendthrift is not carefree, but wounded; and a hoarder is not strategic, but scared. The behaviours that appear irrational often make perfect sense once the emotional backstory is illuminated. A child who once experienced eviction may grow into an adult who cannot part with cash, even when it impairs investment growth. A person who was rewarded for frugality in a family that vilified wealth may unconsciously reject financial abundance to stay loyal to those early values. These are not just habits—they are inherited scripts.

To become aware of these forces, reflection is essential. A useful exercise is to write down three significant financial decisions—positive or negative—and ask: *What emotion was dominant at the time? What was I trying to avoid, prove, or heal? Whose approval was I seeking or fearing?* These questions can reveal surprising truths. They shift the focus from surface logic to deeper drivers. Over time, this practice cultivates *emotional literacy*, the ability to name and work with the feelings that shape financial behaviour.

Cultural storytelling also plays a role in shaping shame and envy. In some cultures, wealth is seen as a sign of divine favour; in others, it's viewed with suspicion. In some families, financial success brings pride; in others, it creates division. Consider the experience of first-generation wealth builders who find themselves straddling two worlds—the one they came from, where money was scarce and relationships close, and the one they now inhabit, where abundance is tinged with guilt or disconnection. Envy from their community and shame from their past can clash, leading to ambivalence or identity fragmentation. Their investment choices may become conflicted—not because they lack skill, but because they lack integration.

Real-world examples help to ground these ideas. When Yvon Chouinard, founder of Patagonia, transferred ownership of the company to a trust and nonprofit dedicated to environmental causes, it was heralded as visionary. But what's often missed is the psychological maturity behind such a move. To choose stewardship over wealth maximisation requires not only clarity of values, but freedom from shame and envy. Had his self-worth been tied to accumulating the highest valuation, the decision would have seemed irrational. Instead, he was able to decouple status from identity and act in alignment with what mattered most.

Contrast this with stories of lottery winners or overnight crypto millionaires who, without the psychological infrastructure to hold such wealth, spiral into destructive behaviours. The issue is not the money—it's the unresolved emotional terrain it activates. Without internal coherence, external gains become destabilising. The same is true in reverse. Financial setbacks can destroy someone not because of the loss itself, but because the shame it triggers collapses their confidence, agency, or sense of identity. Resilience, then, is not merely about risk management—it's about emotional fluency.

From a systems-thinking perspective, it becomes clear that financial behaviour cannot be fully understood without emotional context. Data alone is not predictive. A spreadsheet won't tell you who is carrying inherited guilt, who is compensating for invisible wounds, or who is quietly reenacting family scripts. But if you listen closely—to your hesitation around a certain decision, to the surge of anxiety when someone mentions their bonus, to the irrational rush of relief when you buy something unnecessary—you begin to decode the signals. These signals are not nuisances to suppress. They are invitations to understand.

This understanding is not about perfection. It is about authorship. The moment we recognise how shame and envy operate, we reclaim the power to respond rather than react. We begin to design financial lives that are less performative and more principled. We build structures that reflect our true priorities, not just our inherited pressures. Over time, this creates not only better financial outcomes, but a richer sense of peace and coherence.

The hidden drivers of financial behaviour are not liabilities—they are levers. Once made conscious, they can be harnessed to create alignment, clarity, and resilience. But that requires courage: the courage to look beneath the surface, to feel what is uncomfortable, and to rewrite the narratives that no longer serve us. In doing so, we move from being shaped by our past to shaping our future—with awareness, integrity, and intention.

Chapter 4
Ownership in Action

Ownership, as this book has emphasised from the start, transcends titles or transactions. It is a lens for interpreting the world, a methodology for engaging complexity, and a practice of deliberate action over time. Yet understanding it conceptually is only the beginning. To matter, ownership must manifest in behaviour—it must be enacted through daily choices, embedded in systems, and evaluated not solely by outcomes but by orientation. This chapter pivots from insight to application. It asks the reader to examine not just what they believe, but how they act—especially when no one is watching and when consequences are subtle rather than urgent. Ownership in Action concerns the architecture of daily discipline, the cultivation of environments that reward foresight, and the crafting of decision-making systems resilient to fatigue, distraction, and noise.

People understand that money compounds, yet few appreciate that habits do likewise. Attention, relationships, and even default emotional reactions accumulate in similar fashion. Small, repeated actions over long horizons generate radically divergent realities. Two individuals earning similar incomes but guided by distinct heuristics—one categorising every purchase by utility, the other spending impulsively—will inhabit profoundly different financial, emotional, and cognitive landscapes decades later. The divergence is rarely dramatic; it emerges from invisible iterations. This is the compound effect of hidden choices: subtle, relentless, and ultimately transformative.

To harness this effect consciously requires a personal operating system. And no, this is not metaphorical. High-performing investors, founders, and family stewards all rely on such frameworks: codified, adaptable structures for allocating resources, evaluating trade-offs, managing risk, and reviewing outcomes. These systems are rarely complicated but always deliberate. They reduce decision fatigue, protect mental bandwidth, and buffer against reactive impulses. Tragically, many—often those with substantial assets—depend on hope and habit rather than design, outsourcing clarity to convenience without realising the cost.

The analogy to physical fitness is instructive. We know diet and exercise influence health, yet those who thrive over decades embed routines rather than react sporadically. Financial vitality mirrors this principle. Enduring success emerges not from superior insight, but from alignment: between values, habits, and goals. Knowledge alone is insufficient; systems translate intention into consistent action, creating momentum rather than merely resisting entropy. This chapter presents methods for constructing such systems, drawing from behavioural finance, family governance, and systems engineering.

Another dimension explored is Return on Attention (ROA), arguably more critical than Return on Investment in a world dominated by distraction. Attention is finite, yet often allocated passively—steered by novelty, urgency, and social comparison. Just as capital accrues or depreciates based on deployment, so too does attention. A mind fragmented by notifications or dopamine loops struggles to invest wisely, regardless of knowledge. ROA demands scrutiny: where does cognitive energy flow, and at what opportunity cost? Readers are guided in reclaiming focus, cultivating attentional discipline, and optimising informational intake for long-term gain.

Yet systems and metrics alone are insufficient. Ownership demands emotional range—the courage to face discomfort rather than circumvent it. This includes frank conversations about money with partners, heirs, or colleagues; acknowledging unglamorous trade-offs aligned with core values; and practising delayed gratification not from moralism but from clarity. One illustrative example traces a family navigating inheritance planning across three generations, confronting complexity with transparency, structure, and emotional maturity. Their success hinged not on technical acumen, but on behaviour: choosing ownership over avoidance, stewardship over sentimentality.

This chapter does not prescribe rigid rules; it offers principles and provocations. It challenges readers to move from aspiration to design, transforming intention into habitual practice. Which decisions recur most frequently, and which heuristics govern them? Which default scripts activate under stress, and how might they be re-authored? What does one's calendar, budget, or digital footprint reveal about true priorities?

Framing ownership as a daily practice restores agency. Conventional financial advice often presumes a passive consumer to be nudged or protected. Owners, in contrast, actively shape environments to reflect values and expand capacity. They do not seek control over markets, but mastery over their own processes. Errors occur, inevitably, yet mistakes within a sound system are far less costly than those without one. Systems cannot guarantee success, but they magnify consistency—and consistency is the flywheel of wealth.

There is no ultimate arrival—no perfectly optimised life—but there is increasing coherence, and with coherence comes peace. Ownership is not about maximising metrics; it is about aligning action with purpose over time. This chapter invites readers to embrace that orientation not as an abstract ideal, but as a lived practice, visible in the choices they make, the commitments they track, and the boundaries they uphold.

In the pages ahead, you will explore how to construct a personal operating system, appreciate the compound effect of seemingly minor choices, treat attention as a strategic asset, and confront discomfort rather than evade it. Together, these disciplines form the infrastructure of financial sovereignty. They are not one-off acts, but ongoing practices. And, as with all enduring disciplines, they begin not with knowledge, but with deliberate design. Let us begin there.

Designing Your Personal Operating System –

The modern financial world inundates individuals with options—investment platforms, budgeting tools, tax strategies, and digital dashboards all promising clarity, control, and growth. Yet amid this abundance of choice, many remain overwhelmed, inconsistent, and directionless. The paradox is striking: more tools, less traction. What separates high-functioning individuals and families from the rest is not superior intelligence or access to secret knowledge—it is the presence of a deliberate, well-honed *personal operating system*. This internal infrastructure, while often invisible, governs how they decide, prioritise, and allocate attention and capital across time. And its presence—or absence—is one of the strongest predictors of financial coherence and long-term success.

A personal operating system is not a fixed set of rules. It is a living framework that guides repeated decisions with consistency and alignment. Like the operating system in a computer, it determines what runs, when it runs, and how efficiently it operates. It filters noise, reduces friction, and enforces coherence between intention and execution. Without one, decision-making defaults to emotion, impulse, or imitation. With one, it becomes anchored, strategic, and adaptive. In high-functioning individuals—investors, founders, stewards of multigenerational capital—you find these systems embedded not only in spreadsheets and calendars but in the cadence of conversation, the reflexes of spending, and the narratives they use to explain trade-offs.

The challenge is that most people have never been taught how to design such a system. They inherit fragments—budgeting advice from their parents, investing tips from social media, attitudes shaped by cultural scripts—and attempt to cobble together a coherent strategy. The result is a reactive existence: decisions driven by urgency, peer comparison, or fear of missing out. True ownership begins when one shifts from reaction to architecture. Designing a personal operating system requires intentional choices about how decisions are made, what values take precedence, and how success is measured over time.

One hallmark of an effective system is its capacity to handle recurring decisions with minimal cognitive effort. High-functioning individuals do not revisit the same debates every month—How much should I save? Can I afford this? Should I change my portfolio?—because their system answers these questions by default. For instance, consider the late Jack Bogle, founder of Vanguard, whose investing philosophy—low-cost index funds, long-term holding, and avoidance of market timing—was not merely a preference but a codified system that freed him from the emotional volatility of short-term noise. His discipline wasn't rooted in willpower; it was rooted in design.

The same principle applies beyond investing. Take the case of a family that builds an annual rhythm around money: quarterly check-ins to review their balance sheet, biannual retreats to revisit goals, and a shared framework for categorising expenses as *consumptive, productive*, or *value-aligned.* This structure replaces ambiguity with clarity. It reduces the emotional load of decision-making and turns conversations about money into strategic dialogues rather than reactive negotiations. Over time, these families build not just wealth but wisdom—accumulated through consistent practice, reflection, and refinement.

At the heart of designing a personal operating system is the recognition that values must be operationalised. Most people profess values they do not act on, not because they are hypocrites but because they lack mechanisms. A person who claims to value generosity but gives only sporadically, or who values freedom but maintains no emergency fund, is operating on sentiment, not system. High-functioning individuals translate values into behaviours: allocating a fixed percentage to giving, automating savings, blocking out time for financial reflection. Their systems encode intention into action.

Another essential feature is friction management. Systems must be designed to reduce unhealthy friction—such as the resistance to saving or the temptation to overspend—while preserving or increasing healthy friction, such as the reflection required before making a major purchase. Some families institute a 48-hour rule on non-essential spending above a certain amount, not as a punishment but as a pause—an intentional space between impulse and action. Others create physical and digital environments that reinforce their priorities, from separate investment accounts labelled by time horizon to email filters that block promotional content. *Good design conserves willpower by removing the need for constant vigilance.*

Personal operating systems also evolve over time. What works for a 30-year-old professional may not serve a 60-year-old preparing for legacy planning. High-functioning individuals periodically audit their systems—not just in terms of financial performance but in light of changed values, constraints, or opportunities. They do not treat their systems as dogma but as scaffolding—stable enough to support discipline, yet flexible enough to accommodate growth. They know that a system should not merely preserve the status quo but help surface blind spots, challenge assumptions, and signal when adaptation is needed.

A particularly illustrative example comes from the case of a third-generation family enterprise that had struggled with erratic succession planning and capital allocation. The shift occurred when the family adopted a shared operating system: a governance charter, routine education sessions for heirs, a value-driven investment policy, and regular feedback loops between generations. Within five years, not only had the firm's financial performance stabilised, but intergenerational trust had increased, and decision-making became more decentralised yet coherent. This was not accidental—it was structural. *Systems create culture, and culture sustains systems.*

Of course, system design must also address edge cases: periods of crisis, opportunity, or transition. Here, the strength of an operating system is tested. During a market downturn, does the system default to panic-selling or to rebalancing based on pre-set criteria? During a windfall, does it funnel funds into consumption or align them with long-term goals? During a life transition—a birth, death, or divorce—does it preserve continuity, or does it collapse into disarray? The robustness of a system is measured not by how well it works in ideal conditions, but by how well it preserves clarity amid complexity.

For readers seeking to begin or refine their own system, the starting point is reflection. What are the most frequent financial decisions you make? What principles currently guide those decisions—and where do those principles come from? What behaviours consistently yield outcomes you value, and which ones sabotage your intent? Design begins not with spreadsheets but with self-awareness. From there, architecture can emerge: simple defaults, scheduled reviews, triggers for exceptions, mechanisms for accountability. And, most importantly, a commitment to consistency. *Even a basic system, followed faithfully, outperforms sophisticated ideas applied sporadically.*

As we move further into a world of algorithmic nudges, real-time data, and frictionless consumption, the temptation is to outsource agency—to let technology, media, or trendlines dictate behaviour. But ownership demands authorship. Your financial operating system is not just about efficiency; it is about sovereignty. It is how you say, through action: this is what I value, this is how I decide, and this is the life I am building. Without such a system, even the most informed intentions scatter. With one, even amidst noise and uncertainty, a coherent trajectory becomes possible.

Designing a personal operating system is not a luxury—it is a foundational act of stewardship. It is how intelligent people transform values into results, habits into leverage, and capital into continuity. It is where philosophy meets practicality, and where ownership ceases to be theoretical and becomes a lived discipline. The question, then, is not whether you have a system. The question is whether the system you currently follow was chosen—or merely inherited by accident.

The Compound Effect of Invisible Choices –

Among the most underestimated forces in personal finance is not the market, inflation, or tax policy. It is habit. Specifically, the quiet, often imperceptible habits that accumulate like sediment over years—choices so small they evade scrutiny, yet so persistent they shape entire destinies. When we speak of compound interest, we usually refer to money. But the more profound compound effect is behavioural. Over time, small, repeated actions—each seemingly inconsequential—create exponential divergence. The question is rarely whether someone makes one catastrophic error or one brilliant bet. It is whether their invisible patterns are directionally aligned with long-term advantage or slow erosion.

This is not mere philosophy. Longitudinal studies in behavioural economics, psychology, and even public health reveal the astonishing predictive power of micro-behaviours. The Health and Retirement Study conducted over decades by the University of Michigan illustrates that long-term financial security among similar-income individuals correlates far more strongly with habits than with windfalls or career changes. Regular saving, automatic reinvestment, delayed gratification, and consistency in living below one's means compound over time into an advantage that becomes virtually uncatchable. Not because the actions are dramatic, but because they are repeated without fanfare.

The financial industry often emphasises grand strategy: asset allocation, market timing, tax harvesting. But what silently separates financially resilient individuals is less glamorous. It's how quickly they pay bills. Whether they round up their loan payments. If they check their accounts weekly. Whether they sleep on purchases above a threshold. These actions don't make headlines. Yet the person who invests modestly but consistently over thirty years often outperforms the erratic high-income earner who saves sporadically, spends impulsively, and reacts emotionally to volatility. *Discipline is not only a virtue—it is an accelerant.*

A powerful example comes from the National Longitudinal Survey of Youth (NLSY79), which tracked over twelve thousand Americans from adolescence into middle age. Despite income similarities in early adulthood, those who engaged in consistent financial routines—particularly automatic saving and minimal consumer debt—exhibited dramatically better outcomes across wealth, stress levels, and career optionality. This divergence widened with age. By age 50, many who had seemed 'average' on paper two decades earlier had quietly become what researchers call "stealth wealth" households—financially robust, but without outward signs of extravagance.

One of the most fascinating dimensions of the compound effect is its invisibility in real time. Because incremental change rarely feels consequential, we fail to track its trajectory. Missing one gym session doesn't make you unhealthy. One unnecessary gadget doesn't bankrupt you. But patterns compound. A £4 coffee every weekday is not a crime; it's £20 a week, £1,000 a year. Invested at 7% over 25 years, it's nearly £70,000. But this is not about vilifying coffee—it's about recognising the architecture of habit. *The invisible becomes inevitable when repeated enough times.*

In personal finance, divergence often begins subtly. Two individuals earn the same salary. One begins contributing modestly to a pension at 25, while the other waits until 35. That ten-year head start, even with smaller contributions, can result in a significantly higher retirement corpus due to compounding. But the difference isn't just mathematical—it's behavioural. The early contributor builds a habit of priority; the later one often struggles to catch up because the lifestyle has expanded to match income. Once embedded, spending norms are difficult to reverse. Choices harden into default settings.

Historical examples reinforce this. The famed Framingham Heart Study, though focused on health, inadvertently captured financial data. Participants who reported early adoption of modest financial disciplines—saving first, avoiding revolving debt—tended to enjoy not just better finances but more consistent health outcomes. The reason? Reduced financial stress, greater agency, and more predictable routines. Financial stability, built on invisible decisions, enabled a compounding of wellbeing across domains. Money was not the goal but the infrastructure.

In families, the compound effect often manifests intergenerationally. Parents who model restraint, intentionality, and value-based spending embed a mental model that compounds in their children—not as inherited capital, but as inherited decision-making logic. Conversely, children raised in financially reactive households often absorb emotional scripts around scarcity, entitlement, or avoidance. These become operating systems that dictate adult choices. A 2018 study from Cambridge University found that money habits are largely formed by age seven—not because of formal education, but through repeated observation. *What children see repeated becomes what they believe is normal.*

The institutional world offers parallel insights. Consider S.C. Johnson & Son, a family company with over a century of private ownership. While publicly traded companies often chase quarterly growth, Johnson's operating philosophy has long embraced long-term stewardship. Their decisions—often conservative, deliberate, and aligned with legacy values—have compounded into a culture of durability. These behaviours aren't reactive; they are codified. Similarly, the investment strategy of Warren Buffett is not notable for its complexity but for its patient repetition. His holding periods are measured in decades. His discipline is systematic, not charismatic.

Critically, the compound effect is morally agnostic. It works in both directions. Just as repeated positive behaviours can build resilience, repeated neglect or avoidance compounds fragility. The person who delays retirement planning by five years does not merely lose five years of savings—they lose the compounding effect of those years. The person who avoids tracking their spending doesn't just miss data—they cultivate a tolerance for opacity. And once entropy becomes the norm, reversing it demands disproportionate energy.

To bring this concept into the practical domain, consider the lens of *choice architecture*. What decisions do you make regularly that are not governed by any intentional design? Are your spending, saving, and investing routines the result of deliberate structuring—or inertia? Optimising for the compound effect means reducing the activation energy for beneficial behaviour and increasing the friction for damaging behaviour. It means automating contributions, pre-committing to investment thresholds, using physical or digital constraints to avoid temptation, and maintaining simple, repeatable review cycles.

Ultimately, the compound effect reveals something profound: the trajectory of a life is less about peak moments and more about pattern recognition. Most people overestimate the impact of singular events and underestimate the cumulative force of tiny actions. Financial divergence does not begin with a crisis—it begins with a hundred invisible decisions no one notices. And it is within the power of every individual to shape those decisions intentionally, structurally, and sustainably.

This is not about perfection. No one avoids every unnecessary expense or always maximises every opportunity. But the question is whether the default behaviour aligns with compounding health or compounding harm. Over decades, the small edge becomes the defining gap. Ownership, therefore, is not simply about seizing big opportunities—it is about stewarding the quiet moments. The way you manage a £10 decision echoes across a million-pound outcome. And when your systems support those decisions, when your habits are aligned with your vision, the compound effect becomes not a force to fear—but a force to harness.

Return on Attention (ROA) –

Among all assets a person can manage—capital, time, skill, or social capital—none is as underestimated and undermeasured as attention. It is the foundational input of decision-making, the gatekeeper of learning, and the engine of compounding focus. Yet it is also the most frequently squandered. In a world designed to hijack focus, financial outcomes are increasingly tied not to intelligence or opportunity, but to *attention allocation.* The concept of Return on Attention (ROA) offers a powerful reframing: it is not enough to consider how you spend your money—you must rigorously examine how you deploy your attention.

Traditional financial frameworks teach us to optimise return on investment (ROI), return on equity (ROE), or return on capital employed (ROCE). But behind every investment decision lies the more fundamental question: what were you paying attention to? Were you tracking what matters—or what was merely loud? Were you responding to market signals—or to noise? *Attention is a scarce resource with exponential leverage.* Where it flows, energy follows. And where energy compounds, outcomes diverge—quietly but profoundly.

This is not an abstract theory. Behavioural finance research has repeatedly shown that poor financial outcomes often stem from attentional misallocation. Investors underperform not because they lack information, but because they attend to the wrong signals. In 2007, a landmark study by Brad Barber and Terrance Odean revealed that individual investors who traded the most—presumably those constantly reacting to market news—had significantly worse returns than those who traded infrequently. The difference wasn't analytical capacity. It was attentional distraction disguised as diligence.

Modern life multiplies this risk. The average person now encounters more data in a day than someone in the 15th century encountered in a year. Financial news, opinion feeds, alerts, notifications—all compete for the same neural bandwidth. Yet unlike money, which leaves a clear ledger, attention depletion leaves no trace except decision fatigue and a fractured mind. As psychologist Roy Baumeister has shown, even small cognitive costs accumulate. Just glancing at a screen mid-task reduces subsequent performance. In financial terms, this is akin to losing yield every time you check your phone. *The tax on attention is real—and often invisible.*

At the institutional level, this principle plays out just as forcefully. Long-term capital allocators—from endowments to family offices—are often distinguished not by their access to special investments but by the quality of their filters. They don't chase every opportunity. They are rigorous in what they ignore. The Yale Investments Office under David Swensen was famed for its commitment to a handful of core investment principles—and its systematic disregard for short-term market chatter. Their extraordinary performance wasn't merely a function of strategy—it was a reflection of disciplined attention.

Return on Attention also has profound implications for personal systems. Consider two professionals with similar incomes and cognitive abilities. One spends 60 minutes a day across social feeds, news apps, market updates, and financial commentary. The other devotes that same time to deep reading, strategic thinking, or quiet review of a simple spreadsheet. Over one year, the second person accrues over 350 hours of undistracted attention to high-quality input. That's the equivalent of nine full workweeks directed solely at thoughtful financial and personal decision-making. *The delta in clarity, confidence, and compound wisdom is staggering.*

Crucially, attention is not only about focus—it is also about *discernment.* The ability to determine which signals are signal and which are noise is the defining skill of intelligent ownership. The rise of algorithmic media means we no longer simply choose what to attend to—we are fed what we are most likely to click. This creates what technologists call a "click loop": a recursive narrowing of attention based not on intent but on reaction. Financial media thrives on this. Outrage, panic, and novelty outperform substance. The result is a populace that feels informed but is actually disoriented—rich in data, poor in wisdom.

This calls for a personal attentional audit. What gets your focus before your day even begins? Where do your eyes go during idle moments? How much of your screen time aligns with your actual goals, and how much is a leakage of attention toward low-quality stimuli? The goal is not perfection, but precision. *High ROA individuals are not necessarily monks—they are architects of their attention.* They build barriers to noise and pipelines to signal. They understand that distraction is not neutral—it is negative carry.

The mental health implications of ROA are equally consequential. Anxiety, decision fatigue, and financial paralysis often correlate not with economic reality but with perceived chaos. When attention is fragmented, everything feels urgent. When attention is aligned, even volatility feels navigable. The ability to remain composed amid uncertainty—a hallmark of successful investors and entrepreneurs—is deeply tied to attentional sovereignty. As Naval Ravikant puts it, "The modern struggle is to be rich in peace, not just in assets." That peace begins where attention is reclaimed.

Culturally, we are beginning to see the pendulum swing. Movements such as digital minimalism, intentional living, and deep work are not trends—they are survival responses to the commodification of attention. But few connect this to wealth outcomes. Consider the FIRE (Financial Independence, Retire Early) movement. Beneath the budgeting tips and investment hacks lies a deeper insight: these individuals are reallocating their attention away from consumption cues and toward purpose-defined goals. They are rejecting the default economic narrative and designing their own. That shift is attentional before it is behavioural.

ROA also challenges a core assumption of modern finance—that capital is always the limiting factor. In reality, *attention precedes capital.* The quality of your financial life is often less constrained by money than by the choices you make with the mental bandwidth you possess. And those choices are only as sound as the inputs they are based on. An individual who spends more time researching a mobile phone plan than their pension is not making a rational trade-off. They are suffering from attentional drift. And the cost, while not immediate, is compounding.

To operationalise ROA, one must design for it. This includes tactical changes: disabling push notifications, time-blocking for high-value thinking, using information diets that favour depth over breadth, and building recurring review cycles that nudge awareness toward priorities. But more importantly, it demands a philosophical reorientation: *What is worthy of your attention?* Not just interesting—but worthy. What inputs consistently elevate your judgement, sharpen your values, and align with the life you seek to build?

The deeper insight is that attention is not merely a means to better decisions—it is a reflection of who we believe ourselves to be. When we scatter it, we reinforce a self-image of reactivity and noise addiction. When we channel it, we reinforce discipline, intention, and authorship. High-net-worth individuals are often assumed to have more freedom because of their money. But many of them exhibit a prior mastery: *the ability to direct their attention despite distraction, not because of insulation from it.*

Ultimately, Return on Attention is a meta-skill. It sits upstream of productivity, strategy, and execution. In the same way that return on equity measures how effectively a company uses its resources, ROA measures how effectively a human uses their most fundamental resource: awareness. And like all compounding assets, the earlier it is cultivated, the more profound its impact. The person who can sit with silence, direct focus at will, and curate their inputs with discernment holds a non-linear advantage. Their decisions are cleaner. Their reactions are slower. Their vision is longer. They may not always be the noisiest player in the room—but they are often the owner.

Owning the Uncomfortable –

Most financial frameworks are built to maximise what's visible: yields, returns, ratios, growth. But enduring wealth—personal or generational—is built not just in markets, but in moments of psychological tension and difficult conversation. The skill to endure volatility is widely taught; the courage to confront discomfort rarely is. Yet *the quality of your financial life is directly correlated with your willingness to face what you'd rather avoid.* Ownership, in its deepest form, is not just about assets—it's about agency. And agency begins where avoidance ends.

The avoidance of uncomfortable conversations is one of the most expensive habits in wealth management. Families delay estate planning, not out of ignorance, but because the discussions it requires force them to surface power dynamics, competing values, and emotional legacies. Couples postpone conversations about spending patterns because they would rather preserve short-term harmony than risk conflict in service of alignment. Professionals accept comp packages they don't fully understand because advocating for transparency feels emotionally unsafe. These small evasions compound. What they cost is not only money, but clarity, connection, and control.

The core insight is that *discomfort is not a sign of failure—it is a signal of growth in progress*. When we resist it, we forfeit maturity. When we face it, we activate discernment. Ownership-minded individuals and families understand this distinction. They don't view awkwardness as an obstacle; they treat it as a domain to be designed for. They create systems, language, and rhythms that make space for the uncomfortable—because they recognise it as the raw material of resilience.

Consider the story of the Darvani family, third-generation stewards of a mid-sized logistics business in the Midlands. For decades, the company had been managed with an informal understanding: the eldest son, as in prior generations, would take over upon the father's retirement. But dynamics had shifted. The daughter, Leila, had built the company's e-commerce wing from nothing to 40% of total revenue, and employees increasingly looked to her for strategic guidance. Tensions were growing, but no one addressed them. The father hesitated to confront tradition. The son assumed succession was automatic. And Leila, despite her success, didn't want to appear divisive by raising the issue.

It was only after a facilitated family retreat—proposed by a non-family CFO concerned about mounting confusion—that the real conversation began. Emotions were raw. Assumptions were challenged. But once the discomfort was allowed, clarity emerged.

The siblings agreed to co-lead, with external coaching and a five-year review clause. A governance charter was introduced. Succession became not an entitlement, but a commitment. The business is now stronger. But more importantly, the family is honest. That outcome was only possible because they *owned the discomfort rather than outsourced it to time, silence, or fate.*

Delayed gratification is another domain where discomfort becomes a crucible. It is easy to praise it conceptually. It is harder to practise it in a culture engineered for immediacy. The trade-off between present ease and future value is not just an economic equation—it is a test of internal coherence. Can you resist the appeal of quick wins in order to honour something longer, deeper, truer? That ability doesn't come from willpower alone. It arises from *value clarity*—a commitment to ideals more enduring than impulse.

In behavioural economics, the famous "marshmallow test" has long been cited as evidence of childhood self-control predicting future success. But later research revealed something more nuanced: what matters is not just the ability to delay gratification, but the reason why. Children who believed the experimenter was trustworthy and consistent were more likely to wait. Translation: *delayed gratification depends on an environment that supports trust, not just on individual willpower.* Adults are no different. Ownership flourishes when systems make aligned trade-offs easier, not when they rely solely on heroic discipline.

This principle scales to investment strategy. Owners who build durable portfolios often resist shiny, short-term vehicles that offer high returns but low transparency. They understand that accepting market volatility is more tolerable than accepting structural fragility. That insight is not an investment thesis—it's a psychological posture. It requires being uncomfortable with relative underperformance, public opinion, and the nagging question: "Am I missing out?" The best investors are those who can sit calmly in the pocket of discomfort—because they have already rehearsed their principles.

Owning the uncomfortable also means confronting intergenerational asymmetries. Many families, particularly in cultures where money is taboo, hesitate to speak plainly about inheritance. Children are left unsure of what is expected—or what is fair. Parents avoid disclosure, fearing it will erode work ethic or spark entitlement. But *silence is not neutral—it is a medium in which resentment grows*. The most effective wealth transitions happen when families treat discomfort as part of the design, not a problem to be avoided.

One private wealth advisor in London recalls a client who brought together three adult children and their spouses for what he called "a values audit." The patriarch, nearing 75, had assets well in excess of £60 million but had never discussed distribution. He feared conflict. What emerged in the facilitated session was both confronting and liberating: one child felt he was seen as the "charity case," the other admitted she had no interest in managing a trust, and the third expressed a desire to tie distributions to environmental metrics. These perspectives shocked the father—but clarified the path forward. They co-created a family charter, including clauses that allowed for different asset vehicles aligned to different roles and desires. It wasn't tidy. But it was honest. And that honesty preserved unity far better than politeness ever could.

The irony is that people often avoid the uncomfortable because they assume it will fracture relationships. In truth, it is avoidance that creates the fracture—and honesty that forges trust. As Brené Brown has famously said, "Clear is kind. Unclear is unkind." Financial maturity, then, is not just measured in net worth or tax strategy, but in the willingness to say the unsaid.

Building a life of aligned wealth means developing the muscle of active discomfort. This involves rewiring our assumptions: that tension is not to be eliminated but integrated; that uncertainty is not weakness but wisdom in formation. It also requires updating how we measure success. Too often, we count what is easy to quantify—returns, income, assets—and ignore what matters most: *have I said what needed to be said? have I made trade-offs I can live with? am I proud of how I chose, not just what I chose?*

Owning the uncomfortable does not mean seeking conflict. It means not fearing it. It means becoming the kind of person who can sit with tension without collapsing into blame, defence, or escape. It means acknowledging when clarity is more important than control, when peace requires disruption, and when integrity is worth more than consensus. These are not techniques. They are thresholds. They define the boundary between reactive consumption and intentional ownership.

True owners design not just for outcomes, but for process. They don't just ask "what should we do with the money?"—they ask "what conversations do we need to have before we decide?" That single orientation changes everything. It reframes financial life as a dialogue, not a diktat. It elevates wealth from inheritance to stewardship. And it ensures that what is built is not just profitable, but principled.

In the end, ownership is not defined by paperwork or portfolios. It is defined by the capacity to face what matters, even when it's hard, messy, or uncomfortable. Especially then. Because it's in those moments—when silence would be easier, delay more comfortable, and appeasement more palatable—that real stewardship is forged. And it is precisely that courage that separates those who consume wealth from those who grow it.

Chapter 5
Time as an Asset Class

There is no greater asymmetry in wealth than the command of time. Unlike money, which can be lost and replenished, time is irretrievably spent. Yet, despite this evident truth, both modern finance and productivity culture remain remarkably short-sighted, treating time either as a constraint to schedule around or as a commodity to be optimised, packed, and monetised. This is a fundamental misunderstanding. Time is not a mere backdrop; it is a distinct asset class—arguably the most valuable one at our disposal. How we relate to it often tells more about our actual wealth than any balance sheet ever could.

Those who think like owners do not simply ask, "How much do I have?" They ask instead, "Over what horizon do I exert control?" That subtle shift in questioning signals a profound difference in behaviour, mindset, and eventual outcomes. Transactional actors dwell in immediacy, chasing quarterly gains, daily validation, and the short-lived thrill of instant reward. Owners, by contrast, play the long game—not because patience is innate, but because they grasp the multiplier effect of well-paced decision-making.

Time, in this framework, is not merely chronological. Ancient societies recognised a layered understanding of temporality. The Greeks distinguished between Chronos—the measurable, linear time of clocks and calendars—and Kairos—the qualitative, opportune moment when action has maximum impact. Modern finance has overwhelmingly privileged Chronos, equating speed with intelligence. Yet in strategic contexts, haste often undermines wisdom. Kairos demands discernment over automation, turning attention into leverage rather than mere throughput.

A blind spot in conventional wealth education is the failure to treat time as a consciously allocated resource. We budget capital meticulously but rarely consider bandwidth. We obsess over ROI but seldom examine the return on attention. We ask, "How much will it cost?" more readily than, "How long will it compromise focus or intention?" Distraction, more often than destruction, erodes compounding. Legendary investors—Buffett, Templeton, Li Lu—did not triumph by moving swiftly. They succeeded by mastering strategic patience: the capacity to wait deliberately, absorb uncertainty, and act when conditions, not moods, aligned.

This is no passive waiting. True patience is an active discipline of selective engagement. The seasoned investor, the master craftsman, the elite athlete—they share this trait: the restraint to act only when execution and timing coalesce. Both nerve and self-regulation are essential. The longer the horizon, the less the noise matters—but the harder it is to ignore. That tension differentiates amateurs from professionals, consumers from owners.

History offers vivid illustrations. In 1976, when Jobs and Wozniak launched Apple, the company teetered on collapse due to cash constraints. Many would have pivoted or diluted. Jobs, however, doubled down—not just on capital, but on timing—recognising that a computing revolution depended not on speed alone, but on readiness. Decades later, Apple's enduring success is less about rapid product cycles than its mastery of synchronising design, innovation, and cultural momentum. Kairos, not Chronos, has always been its source of resonance.

Similarly, Baillie Gifford has quietly outperformed faster-moving peers by embracing unusually long holding periods, sometimes exceeding a decade. This approach allows them to weather volatility, reframe temporary underperformance as maturation, and see opportunity where others perceive risk. Their philosophy is deceptively simple: move slowly enough to perceive clearly, act decisively once clarity emerges.

On a personal level, the principle is equally compelling. Time affluence—the subjective sense of having sufficient time—is a strong predictor of wellbeing. Yet many financially successful professionals are chronically time-poor, structuring their wealth around throughput alone. The irony is that money earned through time-sacrifice is often spent to reclaim it: on convenience, luxury, or escape. The solution is not to evade time, but to design it intentionally, proactively, and courageously.

This is the essence of the time-wealth loop: recognising that time and money can be exchanged, but never without distortion or loss. Early retirement, for instance, is rarely about idleness; it is about sovereignty—the ability to cease selling fragments of life to institutions misaligned with one's values. Yet without systems for reintegrating purpose, time abundance can quickly slip into aimlessness. True ownership of time demands more than financial freedom; it requires a personal operating system that clarifies what matters, when, and why.

Designing such a system is not indulgent—it is imperative. Time is the arena in which all other assets manifest. Investments require time to compound; legacies need time to shape; relationships demand time to flourish. The most strategic owners invert the typical question. Instead of asking, "What can I do with money?", they ask, "What can I do with time that money cannot buy?"

That shift transforms everything—from career design to risk management, from parenting to creation, from rest to growth. Slowness, often misjudged as laziness in a culture obsessed with hustle, becomes intentional. Those who craft enduring novels, raise generational families, or build lasting wealth move deliberately. They cultivate roots before seeking height, knowing that deep roots take time and attention.

This chapter treats time not as a mere backdrop, but as an underutilised strategic instrument. We will interrogate cultural myths that warp our perception of time, examine investor mindsets that regard slowness as advantage, and offer frameworks for converting income into autonomy, urgency into clarity, and motion into meaningful progress. We will explore tools for designing lives rich not only in activity but in rhythm and purpose.

Ultimately, time is the great equaliser, the revealer, and the multiplier. It exposes the consequences of attention, the depth of alignment, and the true trajectory of intent. Those who treat time as capital—allocatable, leverageable, and defendable—will not merely accumulate wealth; they will construct lives that compound far beyond the immediately visible. That is the owner's edge. And it begins by claiming time as one's own.

Clock Time vs. Kairos Time –

Modern life is ruled by a single interpretation of time: linear, quantifiable, and accelerating. We live by the clock. Minutes are scheduled, hours are monetised, years are planned in cascading calendars of deliverables and goals. In this worldview, time is not just measured—it is *spent*, as though life itself were a ledger of productivity. But there is an older, richer understanding of time, one that cannot be reduced to metrics or milestones. The Greeks called this *Kairos*: not time as quantity, but time as *quality*—a ripe moment, a meaningful pause, the precise point when action harmonises with context. Understanding the distinction between *Chronos* (clock time) and *Kairos* (event time) is not merely academic. It holds profound implications for how we invest, decide, lead, and live.

The tyranny of clock time is rooted in the Industrial Revolution. With the mechanisation of labour came the mechanisation of life. Factory whistles replaced natural rhythms, and efficiency became virtue. The legacy of this thinking still permeates how we value activity today: speed equals competence, output equals worth, multitasking equals mastery. Yet this conflation of urgency with wisdom is deeply flawed. *Speed often undermines discernment.* In the domains of leadership, investing, creativity, and parenting, moving faster rarely improves outcomes. What matters more is the ability to act *at the right time*—and to know when not to act at all.

Kairos is the architecture of timing. It recognises that not all minutes are equal, not all hours are interchangeable. A conversation held too early falls flat; one held too late fractures trust. A market entry that is rushed burns capital; a delay that is too long concedes opportunity. Kairos is the sensibility that great founders, negotiators, surgeons, and statesmen cultivate: the capacity to read subtle cues, sense inflection points, and align action with underlying readiness. *It's not about doing more, sooner—it's about doing the right thing, precisely when it matters most.*

In financial life, this distinction plays out dramatically. The obsession with daily performance metrics—quarterly returns, real-time dashboards, constant price tracking—keeps investors trapped in a *Chronos loop*, where reacting is mistaken for responding. But the most enduring gains often come not from acceleration, but from discernment. Consider the success of investors like Howard Marks or Li Lu, who are known not for rapid trades, but for patiently scanning the terrain, waiting until conditions reach Kairos—when assets are mispriced, sentiment is misaligned, and structural opportunity emerges. They operate on a rhythm that defies the tick of the market clock.

Long-term wealth builders do not just manage money—they manage timing. They understand that capital gains are often the lagging indicators of correctly interpreted Kairos moments. Missing those moments—not because one lacks data, but because one lacks *discretion*—can create opportunity costs far greater than any fee or tax. The penalty is not just monetary; it is strategic. Misaligned timing compounds errors invisibly. It erodes trust, energy, clarity. Over years or decades, the consequences become vast.

This sensitivity to timing is not reserved for high finance. In family life, too, Kairos carries weight. A parent who works 60-hour weeks may technically "make time" for their child in 30-minute increments. But children do not remember quantity. They remember resonance. A spontaneous walk at the right moment, a conversation when their guard is down, a gesture when it's least expected—that is Kairos parenting. Similarly, a business founder who fires an underperformer three months too late may still "do the right thing" on paper, but the damage to morale and culture is already seeded. *Kairos failure cannot be seen on a spreadsheet, but it is deeply felt in outcomes.*

Different cultures codify this tension differently. In monochronic societies (like Germany, the US, or the UK), time is a fixed resource to be scheduled, partitioned, and adhered to with discipline. In polychronic cultures (such as many in Latin America, Africa, or the Middle East), relationships and context often override schedules. Meetings may start late, but trust is built in the in-between. While neither system is inherently superior, they reflect divergent worldviews: one prioritises efficiency, the other attunement. The question for anyone seeking to build durable wealth and legacy is not which is right, but how to integrate the wisdom of both.

For owners—of businesses, portfolios, or philosophies—the art is to fuse the precision of Chronos with the intuition of Kairos. Calendars and spreadsheets are tools. But insight is earned through presence, awareness, and pattern recognition over time. In practical terms, this might mean declining a lucrative deal that doesn't feel fully formed. It might mean delaying expansion until the right leadership emerges. It might mean initiating a difficult family discussion *before* a triggering event forces it. These are not actions driven by the clock; they are actions guided by clarity.

There is also a personal liberation in embracing Kairos. Clock time often produces anxiety: the sense that one is behind, late, wasting time, running out. But Kairos introduces a more compassionate metric: *alignment over achievement.* It invites the possibility that one can be exactly where one needs to be—even if it looks "off track" by conventional standards. Many late bloomers, second-act entrepreneurs, or early retirees defy Chronos and flourish in Kairos. The author who publishes their first book at 55. The executive who walks away from a company at 38 to raise children. The artist who spends a decade exploring before producing their breakthrough work. *These are not delays—they are ripenings.*

The challenge, of course, is that Kairos requires a different kind of literacy. It is not taught in business school. It is not measured by quarterly reports. It is cultivated through introspection, deep listening, and a respect for unseen rhythms. It demands that we slow down—not as retreat, but as strategy. It also requires courage: the courage to wait when others rush, to say no when everyone says yes, to act decisively when timing reveals its window. *Kairos is quiet, but decisive. It is slow, but consequential.*

This is not an argument against structure. Time still needs scaffolding. But just as capital needs strategy, time needs discernment. The most powerful owners build their lives not just with annual plans, but with Kairos awareness. They learn to ask: *Is this the moment? Is this aligned? Is this fertile?*—questions that cannot be answered by Google Calendar. In doing so, they reclaim time not as something to endure or escape, but as something to *steward.* And in that stewardship lies their edge.

Chronos rewards hustle. Kairos rewards wisdom. Those who master both—who can move deliberately in a fast world—become not just more productive, but more powerful. Because while speed may win sprints, timing governs legacy. And owners, above all, are not here to sprint. They are here to outlast, out-think, and *out-time* the noise.

Strategic Patience –

Strategic patience is not a temperament. It is a skill—a cultivated, practiced discipline of deferral that stands in deliberate resistance to the market's insatiable appetite for immediacy. To act swiftly is to appear decisive; to wait is often mistaken for indecision. Yet in the world of long-term ownership, the most consequential gains accrue not to those who act first, but to those who know precisely when not to act. Patience, when strategic, is not inertia. It is leveraged stillness—an active engagement with uncertainty that is neither escapism nor surrender. It is decision-making by subtraction.

The cultural worship of speed has rendered patience suspect. Business schools teach case studies in bold moves, not deliberate inaction. Markets reward quarterly performance, not generational architecture. And yet, beneath the surface of many enduring successes—be they companies, endowments, or families—lies a quiet but potent principle: *the ability to delay action until the timing serves the mission, not the mood.* Strategic patience is not the avoidance of risk; it is the avoidance of premature exposure. It is waiting not for certainty, but for clarity.

Warren Buffett's investment in Coca-Cola in 1988 is often cited as a model of conviction. Less remarked upon is that he watched the company for decades prior. The buy decision came not from a sudden market event, but from a slow accumulation of insight. The patience wasn't passive; it was deeply informed. Similarly, the French luxury conglomerate LVMH took over 30 years to construct its brand empire—not through rapid expansion but by waiting for undervalued heritage brands to become mispriced opportunities. Their model of patient acquisition favours optionality over velocity, and permanence over volatility.

Strategic patience also thrives in environments where short-term signals are noisy and distorted—environments where immediate action risks being reactive rather than reflective. Consider venture capital. The most successful investors often pass on dozens of opportunities for every deal they make. They understand that their job is not to find the next trend, but to identify enduring value before it becomes obvious. The discipline to wait—to let deals go—is not a constraint, but a competitive edge.

Yet strategic patience requires emotional maturity. The urge to act, to fix, to intervene, is hardwired. Especially in high-stakes environments, the absence of action can feel like a failure to lead. This is a dangerous illusion. In his book *Thinking in Bets*, former poker champion Annie Duke distinguishes between decision quality and outcome quality. You can make the right decision and still lose—and vice versa. Strategic patience operates within this uncertainty. It holds space for outcomes to emerge without rushing the process. It accepts that value and validation may be decoupled in time.

This emotional regulation—the ability to remain calm while others react—is a defining trait of effective stewards. Howard Marks of Oaktree Capital often writes about "patient opportunism": the willingness to wait years for the right investment conditions. When the 2008 crisis hit, Oaktree was liquid, prepared, and swift—because it had been patiently inactive beforehand. It is no coincidence that this capacity to act with speed during dislocation often stems from the prior willingness to wait during stability.

Strategic patience also applies outside finance. In family businesses, those that endure often resist the pressure to chase every growth opportunity. Instead, they focus on culture, continuity, and compounding trust. The German Mittelstand—the network of mid-sized, family-owned firms—epitomises this ethos. Many have survived wars, recessions, and technological shifts not because they acted quickly, but because they moved deliberately. They prioritised intergenerational coherence over short-term expansion. Their pace is their strength.

The same principle governs land stewardship among Indigenous cultures, many of whom manage ecosystems with a 500-year horizon. Strategic patience is embedded in their governance systems—not as a constraint, but as a calibration. Time is not a variable to optimise for speed, but a context to harmonise with. Decisions are judged not just by their immediate outcomes, but by their implications for descendants. This mindset makes patience not only rational, but moral.

Contrast this with the modern investor constantly refreshing stock tickers, or the entrepreneur pivoting every quarter in response to market whims. There is a fine line between agility and distraction. The latter often masquerades as strategy. But high-quality decision-making is not always fast decision-making. It requires intervals of waiting—spaces where ideas can mature, where noise can settle, and where surface volatility does not obscure structural truth.

Importantly, patience must be strategic, not indefinite. Waiting becomes a virtue only when paired with criteria for action. Indecision, disguised as patience, can be just as dangerous as haste. The key lies in defining what one is waiting for: a price, a condition, a partner, a signal. The Japanese concept of *ma*—a conscious pause that gives meaning to action—captures this balance. It is the space between notes that gives rhythm to music. So too in leadership and investing: action without intervals becomes noise; patience without purpose becomes avoidance.

For individuals, cultivating strategic patience requires the design of systems that slow impulse and extend perspective. Decision journals, cooling-off periods, pre-defined checklists—all are mechanisms that convert reactive moments into reflective ones. Financially, this may mean delaying major purchases, extending investment horizons, or resisting the pressure to act on unvetted advice. Psychologically, it requires tolerating ambiguity—not resolving it prematurely.

A telling example comes from real estate investor Sam Zell, who made a fortune buying distressed assets—but only when conditions aligned. During boom years, he would often sit on cash, frustrating partners. But when markets turned, he was ready. His success was not in timing the market perfectly, but in refusing to compromise his standards when others did. Strategic patience granted him not just survival, but asymmetry: the ability to make large moves when others had already spent their dry powder.

Patience also creates leverage—temporal leverage. Those who are not rushed gain optionality. They can negotiate better terms, see patterns others miss, and allocate resources with clarity rather than panic. In a world addicted to instant gratification, patience becomes a competitive moat. The investor who doesn't need to act is often the one best positioned to act when it matters.

This is equally true in personal life. Consider career decisions. Those who rush into roles for short-term gain often pay hidden costs in misalignment and burnout. Those who wait for roles that fit their deeper values—not just their resume—tend to build more resilient, fulfilling careers. Strategic patience is thus not about stalling progress, but about aligning action with intention.

The discipline to wait is, paradoxically, a discipline of movement. It moves decision-making from reflex to reason, from transaction to transformation. It is a meta-skill that governs all other skills: the capacity to distinguish signal from noise, value from price, clarity from emotion. Strategic patience, then, is not a delay tactic. It is the architecture of durable success.

And it is increasingly rare. In markets, politics, and culture, impatience has become a default setting. But those who rewire themselves for strategic timing rather than constant motion build structures that last. They understand that not all returns show up quarterly. Some require cycles, seasons, and silence. They trust not in the speed of their actions, but in the soundness of their reasoning.

Strategic patience is a form of power—but a subtle one. It doesn't shout. It doesn't rush. It doesn't seek the spotlight. It waits, prepares, and then moves with force and focus. The most enduring owners—of companies, of portfolios, of legacies—do not act often. But when they do, they act decisively, because they've waited intelligently. The world rewards those who can afford to wait. But it transforms under those who have trained themselves to.

The Time-Wealth Loop –

Time and money have long been treated as distinct currencies: one counted in hours, the other in digits. Yet in the actual experience of life, they are deeply entwined—each can be used to expand or compress the other. The concept of *The Time-Wealth Loop* invites us to reimagine these assets not as competing forces but as translatable resources, where the wise stewardship of one unlocks richer access to the other. While modern finance obsesses over compounding capital, far fewer ask the more transformative question: *What if we compounded time?*

The assumption that money buys time is both intuitive and, at times, dangerously misleading. The executive who earns enough to outsource every chore may have calendar space, but no mental stillness. The retiree with a seven-figure nest egg may lack the health or relationships to enjoy their freedom. Conversely, the minimalist freelancer who trades down earnings for schedule autonomy may have inadvertently increased their time wealth. *Time, like capital, is not a commodity—it is a context.* Its value depends on how it's experienced, not merely on how much of it is technically available.

Economists and behavioural scientists alike have tried to pin down this elusive relationship. The traditional model suggests that individuals trade time for money early in life (labour) and then money for time later on (retirement). But this sequence is often brittle, rooted in industrial-era assumptions. What's increasingly clear is that ownership—in the truest, fullest sense—means intentionally designing a loop where time and money are in dynamic conversation, not linear exchange. We do not simply earn time at the end of life; we can manufacture it throughout, if we learn to be strategic stewards of both currencies.

This shift begins with reframing time as an asset class. Just as portfolios are constructed around diversification and risk-adjusted return, lives can be designed around optimal time allocation. In this sense, every daily decision becomes an investment—either in acceleration, depletion, or regeneration. We must ask not only what pays, but *what pays in time.*

Consider the compounding effect of micro-decisions. A salaried employee who negotiates for remote flexibility gains not just time from a commute, but access to family moments, higher cognitive bandwidth, and reduced burnout—each of which may translate into better long-term earning potential. A founder who structures their business to run without constant oversight earns dividends in optionality: the capacity to pursue opportunity from a position of calm, not pressure. These are not luxuries; they are engineered advantages, earned through design.

In contrast, poor time allocation corrodes even the most impressive financial gains. This is clearest among high-income professionals whose schedules are colonised by obligations they did not architect. Their attention is fragmented across meetings, their creativity trapped under urgency, their lives lived in after-hours. They have confused wealth accumulation with wealth usability. Without conscious intervention, their money becomes a monument to missed time rather than a mechanism for reclaiming it.

The most time-rich individuals are rarely those who earn the most—they are those who *own their allocation*. They build systems that protect deep work, emotional presence, and strategic thinking. In this light, time becomes a kind of leverage—a multiplier of effectiveness. If money is fuel, time is the engine's ability to convert it into meaningful motion. You can have a full tank and go nowhere fast.

Technology complicates this picture. Productivity apps and digital workflows promise to "save time", yet rarely deliver time we can *feel*. Instead, they accelerate output and increase expectation. The loop is broken: more efficiency leads not to more time, but to more inputs. The question then becomes not just how to earn or save time, but how to reinvest it *deliberately*. This is where time wealth becomes a design problem, not just an income problem.

In elite circles—among founders, portfolio managers, and long-term operators—this philosophy is already in quiet practice. Naval Ravikant, the angel investor and philosopher-entrepreneur, speaks openly about building wealth to "buy your calendar". For him, the apex of success is not having a private jet, but having a Wednesday with nothing on it. Similarly, Warren Buffett famously protects his schedule with monk-like vigilance, understanding that his most valuable resource is *attention unburdened by urgency*. These are not anecdotes of indulgence; they are signals of mastery over the loop.

So how does one engineer a life with high time return? One key is the intentional rebalancing of life's portfolio. Many people treat financial diversification as gospel, yet allocate time monolithically—sacrificing their best hours to meetings or reactive demands. A more effective model borrows from investment strategy: protect time-blocks for high-yield activities (like deep work, health, relationships), hedge against burnout with restorative intervals, and avoid over-exposure to noise. This is not productivity; it is sovereignty.

Another critical element is the choice architecture that supports defaults. Much of time leakage is not due to grand decisions, but to invisible scripts. Email first thing in the morning. Meetings booked without pause. Weekends blurred by notifications. The most time-wealthy individuals *audit these defaults*, then rewrite them. They design workflows that serve their values, not just their outputs. In doing so, they create a flywheel: time buys clarity, clarity improves decisions, decisions create time.

This loop also applies to the household level. High-functioning families, especially multigenerational ones, often operate with shared values around time. They may design collective calendars that honour solitude as much as togetherness. They may co-invest in support structures—like domestic help, financial advisors, or childcare—that convert capital into reclaimed hours. Importantly, they also train their children in the literacy of time ownership, not just money management. This is a cultural compounder, not merely a convenience.

At a societal level, the disparities in time wealth reflect deeper economic inequality. Lower-income workers often face the most rigid schedules and the least margin for strategic patience. The gig economy amplifies this asymmetry by selling flexibility but offering little predictability. To close this gap, time-rich models must eventually become not just elite strategies, but public design goals. Urban planning, workplace policy, and educational systems must begin to recognise *time as a human asset*, not just a scheduling variable.

In practice, building your own Time-Wealth Loop requires reflective tools. Start with a time audit—not just where the hours go, but *what kind of time they are.* Are they controlled or reactive? Focused or fragmented? Regenerative or draining? Next, map your ideal time allocation across four categories: income generation, long-term leverage (e.g. learning, systems-building), health and relationship nourishment, and inner peace. Then interrogate where money could be spent to reclaim high-quality hours—or where overconsumption is converting time into stress rather than satisfaction.

Equally important is the awareness that not all free time is time wealth. Doomscrolling on a couch may be unstructured, but it's not necessarily rich. Nor is filling leisure with errands. True time wealth feels expansive, not idle. It invites the return of craftsmanship, contemplation, and unpressured presence. It is not what you do in the gaps, but what the gaps allow you to become.

As our economies shift from industrial to digital, and from scarcity to surplus, the real scarcity will be not cash, but calm. Not output, but orientation. In this context, those who master the Time-Wealth Loop will not merely be more productive—they will be more *sovereign.* They will think clearer, feel deeper, and act with a patience that outperforms urgency.

Ultimately, wealth without time is ornamental. Time without ownership is wasted. But time with purpose—that is compounding power. That is the loop worth building.

Why the Best Owners Move Slowly on Purpose –

The default posture of modern business culture is urgency. Leaders are advised to move fast and break things. Agility is extolled, speed is conflated with intelligence, and decisions made quickly are often equated with decisiveness itself. But beneath this cultural bias for acceleration lies a quieter, more formidable force: purposeful slowness. The most effective owners—whether of businesses, capital, or time—do not default to rapid movement. They decouple motion from progress and embrace intentional pacing as both strategy and strength. In doing so, they demonstrate that clarity is not a by-product of speed, but its prerequisite—and that the deliberate use of time is itself a form of power.

To move slowly on purpose is not to hesitate. It is not dithering or deferring. Rather, it is to act only when essential, and with the full force of discernment. It is the difference between reactivity and response, between movement and momentum. Warren Buffett's famous dictum—to be fearful when others are greedy and greedy when others are fearful—is not merely an investment heuristic. It is a reflection of this deeper ethic: to operate on a different temporal register than the crowd. Buffett has said that much of his success has come not from being smarter, but from being more patient. Time is his competitive advantage—not just because he uses it, but because he refuses to be used by it.

The discipline of slow ownership begins with clarity. When an owner has a high-fidelity internal compass—defined values, long horizons, and a commitment to stewardship—they are naturally resistant to the noise of short-termism. They do not need to chase the quarterly earnings beat or the latest market fad because they are not optimising for optics; they are optimising for outcomes. Patagonia's decision to "give away" the company by transferring ownership to a trust and non-profit entity shocked much of the corporate world. But to those familiar with Yvon Chouinard's lifelong approach to business, it was not surprising. It was consistent. It was clear. It was not a reaction to market conditions, but the culmination of decades of principle-aligned pacing. Patagonia moved slowly on purpose—so slowly, in fact, that their ultimate move felt to outsiders like a leap. To the company, it was the next logical step.

This form of deliberate pacing is not without cost. Moving slowly demands the courage to withstand ambiguity. It requires enduring the discomfort of not knowing, of waiting without guaranteed reward. For investors, this means holding cash when others are deploying capital. For founders, it means choosing not to scale prematurely, even when the market appears ready. In 2012, Jeff Bezos wrote to Amazon shareholders that "we don't celebrate a 10 percent increase in the stock price unless it comes from the right decisions." His leadership style—relentlessly long-term, tolerant of delayed returns—enabled Amazon to invest billions into infrastructure and R&D without pandering to short-term expectations. In hindsight, these investments look visionary. At the time, they looked slow.

Psychologically, the ability to move slowly on purpose is a function of internal security. Those who are addicted to speed are often compensating for a deeper discomfort with stillness. Activity becomes a proxy for value; busyness masks lack of clarity. But as any seasoned strategist knows, the cost of moving in the wrong direction is higher than the cost of not moving at all. Deliberate slowness, then, is not merely tactical—it is epistemic. It is an admission that wisdom takes time to surface, that complexity cannot be outpaced, and that truly compounding results emerge not from force but from fidelity to process.

Time, in this framing, is not a neutral container. It is a resource to be allocated with care. Great owners treat time as capital—they invest it, steward it, and avoid squandering it on noise. But they also recognise its unique properties: unlike money, time cannot be saved. It can only be spent, or wasted. This asymmetry creates a paradox. The most powerful use of time often looks like inaction. A founder who takes a month to consider a strategic hire, an investor who waits years to enter a position, a family office that spends a decade building intergenerational governance—all appear inactive to the casual observer. But this slowness is not the absence of discipline; it is its highest form.

The benefits of purposeful pacing are not limited to capital. They extend to leadership, relationships, and legacy. The best owners design environments where people can think deeply rather than react quickly, where trust is built through consistency rather than charisma, and where decisions echo over decades. Ray Dalio's Bridgewater Associates, for all its idiosyncrasies, institutionalised reflection through mechanisms like the "pain + reflection = progress" formula. That formula requires time—both to experience failure and to extract insight from it. A fast culture cannot metabolise pain. It can only suppress or bypass it. A slow culture, by contrast, has the capacity to learn.

There is a moral dimension to this as well. The relentless demand for speed often correlates with extractive practices—squeezing workers, burning out founders, overleveraging resources. When owners move slowly on purpose, they create space for ethical discernment. They are less likely to trade long-term trust for short-term gain. They build in buffers, not just in balance sheets but in human systems. The best family enterprises do not simply focus on succession planning; they invest in readiness across generations. This kind of intergenerational thinking requires timelines that cannot be optimised by algorithm. They must be lived.

Slowness also reveals what truly matters. In a culture dominated by urgency, attention becomes reactive. But when one chooses to decelerate, patterns become visible. What once appeared urgent is often revealed to be irrelevant. What was once dismissed as unproductive—deep work, long walks, extended conversations—emerges as essential. As Carl Honoré writes in *In Praise of Slowness*, "There is so much more to life than increasing its speed." The best owners live this insight. They treat time not as a treadmill to be outrun but as a landscape to be cultivated.

Of course, slowness without clarity is merely stagnation. Moving slowly on purpose is not about inertia—it is about agency. It is about choosing the tempo of one's decisions, the depth of one's thinking, and the duration of one's impact. The best owners do not slow down because they are afraid; they slow down because they are focused. Because they understand that leverage comes not from frantic effort, but from aligned action. When time is treated as an asset class—as something to be allocated with intention—it begins to compound. Not just financially, but cognitively, relationally, and ethically.

In markets, clarity is rare. In leadership, composure is underrated. In ownership, pacing is power. And in a world that urges you to move fast, the ultimate act of sovereignty may be choosing to move slowly—on purpose.

Chapter 6
Systems Over Goals

Most people treat wealth as if it were a destination—a sum, a net worth, a lifestyle tier to reach and then inhabit. True owners see it differently. For them, wealth resembles trust or fitness: it cannot be hoarded. It must be maintained, nurtured, and, crucially, re-earned each day through choices, discipline, and deliberate design. In this chapter, we dismantle the seductive myth of "arrival" and turn instead to the infrastructure that sustains enduring success: systems.

The finest owners do not fixate on goals; they construct environments. They refine inputs rather than chase outcomes. A goal is fleeting, a moment in time; a system endures. A well-built system absorbs volatility, adapts, and strengthens—far more reliably than raw willpower or intelligence alone. Sustainable wealth is measured not only by what you do, but by how often you need not decide at all, because the system already has.

Wealth built around goals alone often produces financial abundance paired with fragility. Individuals sprint toward a target, celebrate briefly, then stall, left without reusable momentum. By contrast, those who think in systems cultivate behaviours that render progress habitual, not heroic. James Clear captures this truth succinctly: "You do not rise to the level of your goals. You fall to the level of your systems." Once overlooked in finance, this insight explains why two people with similar income, intellect, and intention can end up decades apart in outcomes—one trapped by reactive choices, the other liberated by invisible, compounding structures.

The first misconception we tackle is The Fallacy of the Finish Line. Believing money itself is the prize ignores far more valuable—though less tangible—assets: autonomy, energy, peace. True wealth is not a number; it is a framework for living well. In this section, we examine how high-functioning individuals and families craft systems that optimise not merely for income, but for alignment. The most potent operating systems are principled as well as efficient, reflecting what matters most, not simply what pays most. Readers will encounter investors who built personal infrastructures to weather both exuberance and despair, and families who created generational guardrails that prioritise stewardship over consumption. You will also be encouraged to scrutinise your own defaults—not for guilt, but for intentional design.

Next comes Mental Automation: Training the Owner's Reflexes. What distinguishes those who act wisely under pressure is rarely superior willpower; it is internalised heuristics—shortcuts cultivated by intention rather than impulse. Like elite pilots or surgeons, seasoned owners operate under constraint with composure. Habit architecture is therefore not incidental; it is foundational. Repeated behaviours—responses to market dips, framing opportunity cost, conversations about family risk—emanate from a mental operating system that is either left to chance or deliberately engineered. Here, we explore what careful design looks like in practice.

From there, we examine Feedback Loops That Make You Richer. Long-term ownership is not about a single correct decision. It is about iterating intelligently. Feedback loops—structures that convert action into learning—distinguish those who plateau from those who compound. Consider a founder who analyses every post-mortem, a family office embedding reflection into quarterly reviews, or an executive who tracks emotional triggers in decision-making as rigorously as financial data. These loops transcend metrics; they cultivate meaning. And more often than not, they are the crucibles of transformation.

We then explore Designing for Optionality—a trait often misunderstood as hedging or indecision, but in truth a cornerstone of resilient strategy. Optionality builds capacity to thrive amid uncertainty. It does not mean acting cautiously, but rather choosing leverage intelligently. Venture capitalists intuitively grasp this: they invest where upside is uncapped and downside contained. The same logic applies to careers, lifestyles, even relationships. Optionality is not a lack of conviction—it is a disciplined preference for adaptability over prediction.

Taken together, these concepts form an invisible architecture of enduring success. They provide a framework that is less reliant on willpower, more aligned with reality, and infinitely more resilient amidst complexity. In a world where change is constant and volatility expected, those who endure will not be the swiftest or boldest, but the owners whose systems absorb disorder and convert it into advantage.

This chapter does not promise fleeting motivation. It offers something more enduring: tools to automate integrity, evolve through experience, and invest in optionality as a form of wisdom. It invites the reader to replace the question, "What should I do next?" with, "What system would make the right next move obvious?"

The shift—from episodic striving to systemised mastery—is not merely a method of thought. It is the hallmark of those who last.

The Fallacy of the Finish Line –

If the finish line of wealth-building were real, it would be littered with exhausted winners. Instead, what we find—across professions, asset classes, and life stages—is that those who chase numbers to a defined endpoint rarely feel they've arrived. They simply recalibrate the target. First a six-figure income, then a seven-figure net worth, then financial freedom by forty-five, then… more. This isn't because people are greedy or broken. It's because the popular metaphor of wealth as a destination is conceptually flawed.

Wealth is not a finish line. It is a system—dynamic, iterative, and self-reinforcing. When individuals orient their lives around reaching a numerical milestone, they adopt a finite mindset in an infinite context. The problem isn't that they haven't chosen the "right number"; it's that they've confused accumulation with architecture. True financial competence stems not from how much you accumulate, but from how well you design systems that keep working—through uncertainty, through setbacks, and long after the original goalposts have shifted.

This fallacy of the finish line is rooted in a broader cultural bias: we overvalue static states and undervalue functional systems. Consider retirement planning. Much of the financial advice industry is designed around achieving a number—the so-called "magic" retirement figure. Yet studies consistently show that many who reach that number either continue working or feel unfulfilled shortly after stopping. Why? Because the number was a proxy for a desired feeling: security, significance, freedom. But the underlying system of meaning—how one uses their time, makes decisions, contributes, or grows—was often never examined.

System design requires a different set of lenses. Instead of asking "How much is enough?" the system thinker asks "How do I want my life to function?" That shift redirects focus from outcome to process. It elevates structure over sentiment. The same principles that underpin durable engineering or healthy ecosystems apply to financial lives: resilience, feedback loops, redundancy, and regular recalibration. The person who masters these is not simply wealthy—they're stable, adaptive, and clear-headed under pressure.

The evidence for systems outperforming goals is abundant, particularly in investing. Consider the contrast between goal-oriented traders and process-oriented investors. Traders who chase specific returns in a given time window often overtrade, misjudge volatility, and suffer from behavioural biases like loss aversion or overconfidence. In contrast, long-term investors like Ray Dalio or the late John Bogle emphasised frameworks—portfolio construction principles, rebalancing rules, decision discipline. Their success wasn't tied to perfect timing or static targets, but to how well their systems absorbed chaos and adapted without emotional overreaction.

High-functioning families often mirror this. In multigenerational wealth studies, the most successful families aren't the ones who hit the highest net worth in a generation—they're the ones who institutionalise values through systems: governance models, decision charters, trust agreements, family constitutions. These instruments help them transcend individual personalities and prevent the erosion of wealth through conflict or misalignment. They understand that wealth without structure is flammable.

The same logic applies at the micro level. Take budgeting. A traditional, goal-based budget might be designed to save £500 a month. A system-based approach, by contrast, embeds that saving into a broader behavioural loop: automatic transfers to separate accounts, spending limits triggered by notifications, reviews scheduled monthly with a spouse or advisor. One relies on willpower; the other on environment design. Systems outperform willpower every time.

But systems thinking requires emotional maturity—especially the ability to delay gratification and tolerate ambiguity. The person who insists on immediate financial results is often impatient not because they lack discipline, but because they are afraid. They fear irrelevance, scarcity, or regret. And so they over-optimise for quick wins. Ironically, it's this very sprinting impulse that exposes them to burnout, poor decisions, and volatility.

In contrast, those who decouple their identity from short-term outcomes can afford to go slow and build well. This doesn't mean they lack ambition. It means they understand that a sustainable edge is built from clarity, not compulsive striving. They track directional progress—via metrics like opportunity optionality, decision quality, or even emotional regulation—not arbitrary benchmarks. Over time, their systems become self-reinforcing.

A telling example is James Clear, author of *Atomic Habits*, who built not just a bestselling book but an intellectual property engine. He didn't merely aim to "write a successful book"; he constructed a system of writing, feedback, iteration, and consistent publishing that made success statistically likely. The book's launch was not a finish line but a milestone in an ongoing system. His model reflects a principle worth underlining: *sustainable success is an emergent property of intelligent systems—not a reward for goal-chasing.*

Another case comes from behavioural finance research. Studies by Terrance Odean and Brad Barber, among others, have shown that retail investors who trade frequently underperform significantly—often by chasing gains or reacting emotionally to short-term market moves. What's striking is that the accounts that performed best over long windows? Often belonged to people who forgot their login credentials. Inadvertently, they created a system: enforced inaction. That passivity, by shielding them from reactive behaviour, became a superior strategy.

There is, of course, a healthy role for goals. Systems don't preclude ambition—they just contextualise it. A goal might act as a compass, helping orient priorities. But it should never be mistaken for the terrain. The terrain is probabilistic, not deterministic. That's why great investors, entrepreneurs, and families revisit their systems more than their targets. They make meta-decisions—about how they decide—rather than obsessing over outcomes they cannot fully control.

Critically, systems also produce a higher return on attention. Goals demand focus only until they're reached, at which point they create either complacency or a craving for the next high. Systems, by contrast, keep attention in motion. They turn financial health into a feedback-rich loop. You don't just learn from what worked—you become better at *seeing* what works, faster.

This shift—from goals to systems—is not merely tactical. It's philosophical. It asks people to define success not as achievement but as repeatable alignment. And that's profoundly empowering, because it removes success from the whims of the market, the media, or the moment. You become someone who doesn't just hope to win—you build a life that keeps winning through better mechanisms, not bigger numbers.

Ultimately, the most successful people don't cross finish lines. They outgrow them. They understand that real wealth is not something you reach; it's something you *run well.* Not just once, but continuously, in rhythm with a system designed to compound clarity, flexibility, and purpose. That is the real race worth running—and designing for.

Mental Automation:

Discipline is rarely the product of superhuman willpower. More often, it's the result of superior design—of internal systems that produce consistent behaviours without requiring constant deliberation. The most effective owners—whether of businesses, portfolios, or personal responsibilities—do not wake up each day negotiating with themselves about what matters. They've architected habits and heuristics that function like embedded code, automating the behaviours that align with long-term stewardship. This is what distinguishes the competent from the compulsive: *mental automation, not motivational flair.*

Mental automation refers to the strategic encoding of key decisions into repeatable patterns. These are not mindless routines but intelligent defaults—designed reflexes that reduce friction, protect bandwidth, and preserve integrity. In ownership, this becomes critical. Every decision carries potential compounding effects, which means every micro-misstep has a macro-cost. Owners who must re-evaluate every choice from scratch are not only slower—they are also more vulnerable to emotion, fatigue, and inconsistency. Mental automation protects against that erosion.

Consider the heuristic used by Warren Buffett: "Would I be happy to own this business if the market shut down for 10 years?" This simple reflex guards against short-termism. It doesn't require deep analysis each time—it filters decisions before they consume cognitive resources. Or take Ray Dalio's personal decision rule: when in doubt between two paths, choose the one that will develop you the most. Such principles aren't high-concept abstractions—they are tools for mental compression. *Great owners think in packets, not in paragraphs.*

Automation starts with awareness. One cannot automate what one hasn't made explicit. Ownership-oriented individuals begin by mapping their high-frequency decisions: how they spend, how they respond to volatility, how they manage time, how they negotiate with others. They identify the leverage points—places where a single behaviour, repeated consistently, yields asymmetric benefit. Then, they design *defaults*: pre-committed responses that align with their values and objectives. These might include "no meetings before noon without strategic purpose" or "investing a fixed percentage of income regardless of market conditions." The power lies not in their novelty, but in their consistency.

The psychology behind this is well-supported. In behavioural science, the concept of implementation intentions—pre-deciding what action to take in specific contexts—has been shown to significantly improve follow-through. Saying "If X happens, I will do Y" reduces the cognitive load at the moment of choice and increases the likelihood of alignment between intention and action. In financial contexts, this is gold. Automated savings, threshold-based investing, blackout windows for impulsive purchases—these are not signs of rigidity but of strategic constraint. *Freedom lives inside good fences.*

Cognitive bandwidth is not a renewable resource. Decision fatigue is a silent enemy of good ownership. The more high-stakes choices a person must make each day, the more likely they are to default to expedience over principle. This is why many high-functioning leaders aggressively standardise low-stakes routines—what they wear, when they eat, how they start their mornings. It's not eccentricity; it's economy. By automating the trivial, they protect their finite attention for what truly matters. Ownership, when practised intentionally, demands this form of internal triage.

Habits are the behavioural output of automated thinking. But not all habits are created equal. Ownership-aligned habits are distinguished by two features: *they reinforce identity, and they compound integrity.* A founder who begins each week by reviewing key metrics not only maintains control—they remind themselves that they are accountable. A household that meets monthly to review spending patterns is not merely tracking money—they are reinforcing shared values. Over time, these rituals stop being tasks. They become *embedded logic*, guiding behaviour even in the absence of oversight.

The challenge lies in initial setup. Automation requires upfront investment: in designing the right defaults, testing them, and revising when necessary. It's tempting to rely on motivational spikes instead—to act when inspired, to defer when distracted. But reliance on mood is the enemy of ownership. Owners act according to principle, not impulse. And so they build systems that function whether or not they feel like it. This is not dehumanising—it is dignifying. It honours the complexity of life by refusing to let transient emotions override enduring commitments.

Mental automation also protects against overreaction. In volatile contexts—market crashes, business crises, interpersonal conflict—

those without decision protocols tend to lurch between extremes. The owner with clear operating principles remains centred. When the market drops 20%, they refer to their "downturn playbook." When a team member underperforms, they consult their feedback framework. They are not paralysed by uncertainty because they have *pre-committed to clarity.*

Take the example of a technology executive who, during rapid company growth, found herself making the same half-dozen types of decisions weekly: hiring, prioritisation, investor communications, delegation. Rather than treat each instance as unique, she documented decision templates—questions to ask, variables to weigh, trade-offs to consider. Within months, she had converted decision-making from a reactive burden into a structured, coachable process. Her team followed suit. The company's pace didn't slow—but its clarity improved. *Mental automation scaled judgement across time and people.*

There is a moral component to this as well. Defaults shape not just efficiency but ethics. The person who automates charitable giving each month is not just being organised—they are encoding generosity into their system. The family that builds a practice of sharing financial decisions with teenage children isn't just being transparent—they are raising future owners. Automation can reinforce or corrode values, depending on what's chosen. This is why reflection is non-negotiable. The worst systems are those that run on assumptions never examined.

Feedback plays a crucial role here. Automation must evolve. The owner's reflexes need periodic recalibration. What worked at one stage of life or business may become maladaptive later. The investor who once thrived on risk tolerance may, after a major loss, need a new risk profile. The founder who once needed to micromanage may, at scale, need to unlearn that reflex. Effective owners build review loops into their systems—monthly retrospectives, quarterly audits, annual sabbaticals—not as indulgences, but as strategic hygiene. *Mental automation that isn't regularly updated becomes mental rigidity.*

Training the owner's reflexes means designing for repeatability without compromising adaptability. The best systems are those that allow for nuance within structure. They don't eliminate discretion—they elevate it. By offloading the trivial and standardising the routine, they give owners the space to apply discernment where it truly counts.

This is what separates amateur operators from durable owners. The former react; the latter rehearse. They don't rely on the randomness of emotional energy or external validation. They rely on systems, protocols, heuristics, and rituals that *run the right play—even when the spotlight's off.* In doing so, they build institutions—not just incomes. They reinforce character—not just cash flow.

Ultimately, ownership is less about what you control and more about how consistently you control yourself. Mental automation, thoughtfully constructed and periodically refined, is how that consistency is achieved. Not through force. Through architecture. Through rhythm. Through trust in a system that you built—consciously, purposefully, and in alignment with the future you're committed to owning.

Feedback Loops That Make You Richer –

Success, when properly dissected, is rarely a product of genius in isolation. More often, it's the result of a well-calibrated system—an individual or organisation capable of translating feedback into strategy with high fidelity. At the heart of every durable form of ownership is a loop: a recursive, responsive structure where actions generate data, and data shapes future actions. Whether in investing, business, or personal finance, *the ability to build and refine these feedback loops is one of the most underrated financial advantages of the modern age.*

Feedback is not simply information. It is processed, interpreted, and applied signal. This distinction matters. Many people are exposed to experience, but few truly extract learning. They confuse activity with progress, repetition with refinement. Owners think differently. They do not assume that outcomes—whether success or failure—speak for themselves. Instead, they interrogate them. What worked? Why did it work? What part was luck? What was replicable? *The owner's mind is trained not just to act, but to learn from acting.*

This mindset is fundamental to adaptive systems thinking, which differs from linear thinking in one crucial respect: it expects error and builds mechanisms for recovery. While linear systems seek optimisation in static environments, adaptive systems thrive on iteration. They are dynamic by design. They do not aim for perfect decisions, but for *improvable ones*. This is the core of strategic ownership: creating structures that become more intelligent with use.

Entrepreneurs often exemplify this best. Consider the early years of Stripe. The Collison brothers didn't simply launch a payments company—they launched a perpetual testing engine. Every friction point for developers became a prompt for redesign. Every failed integration wasn't just patched—it was logged, analysed, and used to rewire the onboarding process. Over time, their internal feedback loops became a competitive moat. They could improve faster than others could copy. *Feedback became fuel.*

Or take the example of Sara Blakely, the founder of Spanx. Her success wasn't linear. She was rejected by multiple manufacturers, questioned by advisors, and underestimated by analysts. But she built her empire on a rigorous loop of trial, error, and revision. Every product was refined based on direct customer insights. Every marketing misstep led to sharper positioning. She credits much of her growth to a habit developed in childhood—her father would ask her at dinner, "What did you fail at today?" The goal wasn't shame—it was *iteration as identity*.

The best feedback loops are not merely responsive. They are *designed*. They involve three core components: a system for capturing meaningful data, a routine for processing it, and a structure for acting on it. Each of these elements can be applied personally or organisationally.

First, *capture*. Owners build rituals that record reality without bias. This might be a monthly financial review, a portfolio journal, a team debrief, or a customer sentiment tracker. Without data—quantitative or qualitative—patterns remain invisible. And without consistent collection, those patterns remain anecdotal.

Second, *processing*. Here, the emphasis is on interpretation. What story is the data telling? Are we learning the right lessons or reinforcing confirmation bias? Critical thinking is essential. So is contrast—comparing similar situations over time, or inviting external perspectives to challenge assumptions. This is where advisors, mentors, and even rivals can function as part of the loop—not to dictate action, but to sharpen insight.

Third, *action*. Learning without application is mental decoration. Feedback must drive behavioural shifts—whether in investment strategy, business operations, or personal budgeting. But the best owners go further: they document the learning. They codify it into policies, playbooks, or heuristics that raise the system's baseline intelligence. *Over time, the system itself becomes a teacher.*

Investors who compound wealth most reliably are rarely those with the most brilliant theses. They are those with the most honest feedback mechanisms. Ray Dalio institutionalised this principle at Bridgewater through radical transparency and idea meritocracy. Every meeting was recorded. Every idea was rated. Feedback was not optional—it was the circulatory system of the firm. While the model may not suit every context, the underlying logic is sound: *organisations—and individuals—either metabolise feedback, or they calcify.*

Too many high-performing professionals make the mistake of treating feedback as episodic. They request it during performance reviews or post-mortems. But for owners, feedback must be *continuous, ambient, and self-initiated.* It is not what happens when things go wrong—it is what happens *always*. It is the pulse-check, the mirror, the compass. And it must include both positive reinforcement and constructive correction. Knowing what not to repeat is valuable; knowing what to repeat with confidence is *essential.*

There is also a cultural layer here. Systems thinking invites a shift from ego-based evaluation ("Was I right?") to process-based evaluation ("Was the process sound?"). This removes moralism from mistakes and replaces it with *engineering logic.* When a founder loses a deal or makes a bad hire, the right question is not "What's wrong with me?" but "Where in the system did the signal get missed?" This depersonalised accountability encourages faster recovery and *stronger system upgrades.*

Feedback loops that make you richer—financially, intellectually, and ethically—are those that close. An open loop is one where signal enters but is never applied. This leads to information overload, not wisdom. A closed loop takes insight, acts on it, and then observes the result of that action. Over time, these loops create *compound insight*, which is more valuable than compound capital. It's the reason some individuals in their 40s have the decision-making precision of others in their 70s—*they've run more loops.*

Importantly, not all loops operate on the same timeline. Some feedback arrives instantly—like a stock price reacting to news. Other feedback arrives slowly—like the outcome of a business pivot or the consequence of lifestyle decisions. Adaptive owners respect this diversity. They create short, medium, and long-cycle review structures. They don't overcorrect based on noise. But they don't ignore the signal when it finally arrives either.

One powerful example of this is Jeff Bezos's "regret minimisation framework," a personal mental model that shaped his decision to leave his stable hedge fund job and start Amazon. While not strictly a feedback loop in operational terms, it reflects a meta-cognitive form of feedback: learning from the imagined future. Bezos ran the loop in reverse, asking what his 80-year-old self would want. This kind of foresight is not guesswork—it's anticipatory feedback, the use of future regret as present signal. *Great owners think across time spans.*

At the micro level, feedback loops improve execution. At the macro level, they shape identity. They allow an owner to say not just "I made better decisions," but "I became someone who makes better decisions by default." This is what distinguishes transient success from enduring mastery. Systems thinkers don't just seek wins. They seek *understandable wins*—victories that can be reverse-engineered, repeated, and eventually delegated or scaled.

Financially, the impact of this orientation is significant. Owners who run disciplined loops are more likely to cut losses early, double down on strengths, and avoid overreaction. Their risk management improves not because they take fewer risks—but because they *learn faster per risk taken.* Entrepreneurs who learn from their third failed pitch what others only learn by their thirtieth raise capital more efficiently. Investors who track their decision process—not just their outcomes—build portfolios that express intention, not impulse.

Ultimately, feedback loops are a humility mechanism. They acknowledge that no decision is perfect, but every decision can teach. They convert experience into capital, and capital into judgement. For thoughtful owners, that is the real compounding engine. Not just money growing over time—but *wisdom growing with it.*

Designing for Optionality –

Most people structure their lives and portfolios for what they expect. Owners design for what they can't see coming. *Optionality is not about prediction—it's about preparation.* It is the deliberate creation of flexibility in a world that punishes rigidity and rewards adaptive advantage. While traditional financial planning often assumes a knowable future, the owner mindset assumes contingency. The question isn't merely "What is my goal?" but "What if things change?"

In financial and life strategy alike, optionality refers to the ability to pivot, reallocate, or respond without disproportionate cost. In systems terms, it is a form of embedded resilience. An optional life design doesn't resist volatility—it metabolises it. This is not the same as indecision or over-diversification. It's an architecture of intention that values leverage, not clutter. Done right, optionality protects downside while preserving the potential for asymmetric upside.

Venture capital is perhaps the purest institutional expression of this principle. A typical venture portfolio is explicitly constructed on the premise that most investments will fail or underperform, but a small minority will drive the fund's return profile exponentially. This is not tolerated—it is *designed.* Every decision in VC, from cheque size to board participation, is shaped by an understanding of convexity: limited downside, open-ended upside. The best VCs don't just pick companies—they pick optionality. They back founders who can navigate pivots, expand market surface area, and adjust business models without collapsing the company's coherence.

Take Bessemer Venture Partners, one of the oldest VC firms in the United States. Their "anti-portfolio" famously documents the wildly successful companies they passed on—Apple, Google, Airbnb—not as a marketing gimmick, but as a reflective practice. It reveals an essential truth: *you can't always pick the winners, but you can build a system that keeps you in the game long enough to catch one.* Optionality is that system.

The same thinking applies outside venture. In life design, optionality might mean preserving geographic mobility, maintaining broad networks across industries, or developing multidisciplinary skills that can be redeployed as technology reshapes work. For individuals, optionality is often found not in more choices, but in better *structured* ones—decisions that preserve the ability to respond to information over time. Owning a small business with digital leverage, for instance, may provide far more optionality than being a highly paid executive on a narrow corporate track.

The key lies in recognising that optionality is less about adding more options and more about avoiding irreversible commitments that limit future agency. A common financial trap is lifestyle inflation—converting liquidity into fixed cost. High-earning professionals may find themselves locked into a mortgage, school zone, and career path that looks affluent but is structurally brittle. Their decisions, while seemingly smart at the time, reduce room for manoeuvre. *Optionality erodes quietly.*

This is where defaults and design intersect. Owners design decisions that preserve optionality by default. A portion of capital remains unallocated, ready to be redeployed. Time is blocked not just for known commitments, but for unexpected opportunity. Relationships are nurtured beyond current utility. These are not defensive hedges; they are strategic reserves. They create capacity—not just protection.

Philosophically, designing for optionality also requires relinquishing the fantasy of total control. This is its paradox. The best plans are not those that foresee all outcomes, but those that remain *functional under a range of outcomes*. Nassim Taleb, whose work on antifragility is central to this thinking, argues that optionality is one of the only free lunches in finance—it allows you to benefit from uncertainty without having to predict it. But optionality is only valuable if it is *accessible*. Owners convert optionality into advantage by having the capital, clarity, and confidence to act when others are paralysed.

Consider how Amazon structured its cloud computing business, AWS. Originally built to support Amazon's own internal infrastructure, it wasn't conceived as a standalone product. But by architecting the system modularly and retaining internal optionality, they were able to externalise it when they noticed demand. That single decision—keeping the design open-ended—spawned a business unit that now drives the majority of Amazon's profits. It wasn't foresight. It was *option-aware design.*

On the personal level, the same logic applies to career architecture. Take the example of Reid Hoffman, founder of LinkedIn. His career evolved from academia to entrepreneurship to venture capital—not through haphazard moves, but through a mindset of compound optionality. By investing early in both people and platforms, he preserved access to high-quality opportunities and gained exposure to evolving ecosystems. Importantly, his career decisions were often *non-maximising in the short term*—he took roles at companies like PayPal where the experience and network were more valuable than the salary or title. *Owners prioritise leverage over optics.*

Optionality also has a psychological component. It supports a calm confidence that comes not from certainty, but from contingency. People with optionality sleep better. They can absorb shocks, say no to bad deals, and wait for the good ones. It is an antidote to both fear and FOMO—because it reinforces agency. Not the illusion of control, but the reality of *adaptive positioning*. Optionality, in essence, is the financial and existential version of compound interest—it may not feel urgent, but over time, it outperforms.

Importantly, optionality is not a substitute for commitment. It is a complement to it. Some decisions must be all-in. A marriage, a business partnership, a high-conviction investment—these require a different kind of thinking. But even these can be approached with intelligent safeguards. Ownership does not mean avoiding exposure; it means managing it intentionally. Great founders don't avoid risk—they *structure it.* Optionality allows them to place big bets while preserving the ability to navigate or course-correct when required.

The question for readers is not whether they *have* optionality, but whether they are *cultivating* it. What percentage of your time, capital, and attention is invested in things that expand your future freedom? What aspects of your portfolio, career, or life design are too rigid, too path-dependent, too exposed to a single outcome? These are uncomfortable questions, but essential ones. Because in a world of accelerating change, optionality is no longer a luxury. *It is strategy.*

And strategy, in the owner's world, must be expressed not just in plans but in systems. Systems that leave room for serendipity. Portfolios that include asymmetric bets. Calendars with white space. Relationships that aren't purely transactional. Optionality isn't abstract. It's architectural. And like all good architecture, its value reveals itself over time—especially when the weather changes.

Great owners are not the fastest movers, the best predictors, or even the most decisive. They are those who build conditions that *remain advantageous in motion.* Optionality is their hidden discipline—the silent margin that turns volatility into growth, distraction into selectivity, and complexity into advantage.

Chapter 7
The Emotional Balance Sheet

There is no ledger entry for fear. No column that captures shame, joy, or longing. Yet every financial choice—from the smallest daily transaction to the largest capital allocation—is guided, often invisibly, by emotion. Most people assume they act on logic. In truth, they make emotional wagers cloaked as reason. The true risk is rarely the market; it is misreading ourselves.

Chapter 7 confronts what conventional finance ignores: that our emotional landscape is not peripheral to wealth, but central. We do more than manage capital; we metabolise meaning. Beliefs about worth, safety, sufficiency, even identity, underpin every financial move. To think like an owner, we must also feel like one—not haphazardly, but intentionally; not reactively, but reflectively.

This chapter maps the interior terrain that shapes external outcomes. It reframes emotional capacities—gratitude, forgiveness, joy, release—not as sentimental indulgences but as structural levers. These are not "soft skills." They are disciplines that determine whether we hoard, invest, or squander our life energy. They explain why a person with financial freedom can feel impoverished, while another with modest means can live with remarkable clarity. Numbers, as it turns out, rarely tell the full story.

Take gratitude. Often miscast as a passive afterthought, owners practise it proactively. Gratitude regulates impulse, prevents overreach, anchors decisions in sufficiency, and steadies the nervous system amid volatility. Behavioural finance research shows that grateful individuals display greater patience and are more willing to defer gratification—a clear advantage in markets. One private equity partner recounted that during the 2008 crisis, it wasn't models that kept him steady but his morning ritual of handwritten gratitude entries. "It reminded me we had enough runway. That I wasn't making decisions for my ego," he said. "It saved me from a few very expensive mistakes." His spreadsheet didn't capture it, but his emotional balance sheet did.

Forgiveness operates differently, yet no less powerfully. Financial regret—haunting past investments, missed opportunities, ventures started too late or never at all—can calcify into cynicism or recklessness if unprocessed. Forgiveness is not moral absolution; it is an operational reset. It frees mental bandwidth, allowing lessons to be learned rather than loops repeated. Drawing on practices like narrative reprocessing and self-distancing, this chapter explores how owners release emotional debt without discarding wisdom. What we fail to metabolise, we repeat. Forgiveness, far from weakness, sharpens clarity.

Then there is joy, often misunderstood in economic life. Frequently conflated with novelty, dopamine highs, or performative luxury, genuine joy has a subtler signature: calm, grounded, enduring. Owners distinguish fleeting excitement from durable alignment. When harnessed effectively, joy functions as a compass, signalling what resonates rather than merely excites. The most enduring financial decisions are rarely made from fear or hype; they emerge from a felt sense of internal consonance. The entrepreneur who declines funding to preserve autonomy, the family that simplifies life to reclaim time—these are not downgrades, but strategic reallocations, reflecting a valuation model that factors in meaning alongside returns.

Perhaps the most emotionally intricate skill of ownership is knowing when to let go. Exiting a business, relinquishing leadership, or selling a cherished asset cannot be reduced to valuation metrics alone. These moments demand a different sort of wisdom: Am I holding on because it is still generative, or because I fear the act of release? Founders often linger—not out of greed, but attachment: the enterprise embodies identity, the team represents legacy. The exit feels like erasure. Yet astute owners understand that letting go can be the highest expression of stewardship. One founder, after declining three acquisition offers, accepted a modest deal. "It was time," he said. "Not because I couldn't push harder, but because pushing further would have been for the wrong reasons." That, too, is ownership.

This chapter offers not emotional instruction but emotional architecture—a framework to audit the unseen forces shaping how we hold money, power, and choice. The emotional balance sheet includes more than assets and liabilities: it accounts for capacity, resilience, and perspective. Owners who manage this well do more than accumulate wealth; they wield it with integrity.

Ultimately, wealth is never a cleanly calculated output. It is the residual of thousands of emotionally charged decisions. Learning to see and shape the emotional infrastructure behind those choices is not optional. It is foundational. The stock market may behave rationally in the long term. We are not spreadsheets. And the long term, as always, is built one feeling at a time.

Gratitude as Capital

Gratitude is often dismissed as an afterthought—a soft, sentimental emotion best reserved for personal relationships, mindfulness retreats, or occasional journal entries. But this underestimation betrays a profound misunderstanding. *Gratitude, properly cultivated, is not an accessory to rational decision-making—it is a form of cognitive capital.* It reshapes attention, alters risk perception, and serves as a stabilising force amid volatility. For owners—those who think in terms of stewardship rather than accumulation—gratitude is not a feeling. It's an input.

Much of modern decision-making architecture, particularly in finance and leadership, rewards hyper-vigilance. Scarcity, not sufficiency, is the assumed lens. Markets move on fear, and the systems built around them do too: quarterly reporting, performance incentives, algorithmic alerts. In such an environment, gratitude becomes countercultural. But *that is precisely why it has power.* Gratitude interrupts reactivity. It acts as a psychological buffer, curbing the urgency to optimise every variable, acquire every asset, and control every outcome.

The neuropsychological evidence is strong. Studies by researchers at the University of California, Berkeley, and Harvard Medical School have shown that gratitude practices measurably reduce cortisol levels and increase activity in the prefrontal cortex—the brain's executive control centre. *In plain terms: grateful people make better long-term decisions because they are less emotionally hijacked by short-term volatility.*

A private investor once described how a daily habit of listing three things he was genuinely grateful for—not goals achieved, but states appreciated—created what he called "a soft ceiling" against panic. "When the market nosedives, the default is fight or flight," he explained. "But if you've trained your mind to recognise what you already have, the perceived loss isn't existential. That changes how you respond." He noted that during the 2020 market shock, his gratitude practice didn't just improve his emotional wellbeing—it affected portfolio performance. He didn't dump quality assets under pressure. He stayed the course. And he profited.

This anecdote is neither isolated nor incidental. It points to an under-discussed but fundamental truth: *emotions drive capital flows*. The illusion of the rational investor persists in theory, but behavioural economics has long dismantled it in practice. Gratitude, unlike greed or fear, widens the frame. It shifts the focus from what is lacking to what is working. It reorients the decision-maker from a deficit mindset to a position of enough—and this subtle pivot changes everything.

Consider how gratitude reshapes our relationship with consumption. Without it, every financial decision becomes a referendum on status, security, or self-worth. We spend to signal. We invest to prove. But when gratitude is present, the same decisions take on a different tone. There is less anxiety in the trade-off, more awareness in the choice. We stop confusing abundance with accumulation.

A high-functioning family office in New York has embedded gratitude formally into their investment committee meetings. Before discussing allocations or asset performance, each member shares one thing they're grateful for—personal or professional. The exercise lasts five minutes. It's not for morale. It's structural. The managing partner explained, "It reduces status anxiety in the room. It softens the ego-driven posturing. We make better decisions because we're less defensive." Over a decade, their investment performance has outpaced their peers not just in returns, but in portfolio durability—

fewer panicked pivots, better manager relationships, more coherent long-term bets.

The logic of gratitude-as-capital becomes even more pronounced when contrasted with fear-based decision-making. Fear distorts time. It accelerates the present and catastrophises the future. Gratitude, by contrast, slows cognition. It expands the capacity to perceive nuance. *This is not sentimentality—it is strategic cognition.* Fear narrows the aperture. Gratitude widens it.

This matters not just in markets but in life architecture. People driven by fear build brittle lives: over-leveraged schedules, reactive commitments, transactional relationships. Their time is colonised by "what if." Gratitude offers a recalibration. It grounds the person in what is already working—health, friendship, competence—and thereby provides a more accurate base from which to assess risk or opportunity. It is no coincidence that many of the best capital allocators—Buffett, Munger, Dalio—emphasise psychological resilience and inner stillness as prerequisites for clear thinking. Gratitude is not all of that. But it is a gateway.

To be clear, this is not about forced positivity or toxic optimism. Manufactured gratitude—where one feels compelled to "be thankful" as a form of denial or spiritual bypassing—is counterproductive. *True gratitude is discerning, specific, and grounded in observation.* It does not deny difficulty. It contextualises it. When practised authentically, gratitude reveals surplus where we thought there was none. That surplus—of trust, of capability, of resourcefulness—can then be reallocated consciously.

There's also a systems dimension worth noting. People who operate from gratitude tend to build different kinds of systems. They favour sustainability over exploitation, redundancy over efficiency, interdependence over extraction. These design choices matter. Over time, they lead to institutions—families, firms, communities—that are not just resilient but *regenerative.* They produce more than they consume. Not coincidentally, these systems tend to outperform. They attract talent, retain trust, and ride out turbulence without losing internal coherence.

Gratitude also changes how we relate to goals. In a scarcity paradigm, goals are often driven by inadequacy: to fix, prove, or outrun. Gratitude, by contrast, allows goals to emerge from aspiration rather than desperation. This makes them more durable. The person who builds out of appreciation builds differently than the person who builds to compensate. The architecture may look similar from the outside, but the stress lines show up under pressure.

A venture capitalist once reflected on why he passed on several high-profile unicorns that later imploded. "At the time, I couldn't fully articulate it," he admitted. "But something felt off. The founders were chasing ghosts. They weren't building out of conviction—they were building out of emptiness." Gratitude, he realised in hindsight, might have acted as a filter: a signal for whether a team was grounded enough to endure. "The ones who had some form of gratitude practice—however informal—tended to be clearer, calmer, and more adaptive. That's the stuff you can't model, but it matters."

All of this points to a core proposition: *gratitude is not a reward for success. It is a prerequisite.* It shapes how we define success in the first place. It stabilises our nervous systems. It sharpens our perception of value. And it cultivates an inner baseline that makes ownership—true, grounded ownership—possible. Gratitude is not the opposite of ambition. It is what ensures ambition doesn't become pathology.

In financial life, as in personal life, the quality of our decisions is inseparable from the state of our nervous system. Gratitude steadies it. It turns noise into signal. It doesn't make markets less volatile or life less complex—but it makes us less compulsive within them. For the owner who aims to build not just wealth but coherence, not just returns but resilience, gratitude is not decoration. It is foundation. It is capital in its most unrecognised and undervalued form.

Forgiveness of Financial Regrets

Most people carry more than just numbers in their portfolio—they carry narratives. Regrets, shame, what-ifs, and silent recriminations over financial decisions made in moments of inexperience, fear, or exuberance. The pain of a mistimed investment, the weight of a missed opportunity, or the lingering echo of a poor spending decision doesn't simply fade with market recovery. It calcifies into hesitation, shapes future risk tolerance, and quietly erodes clarity. Forgiveness of financial regret is not about absolution from fault—it's about recovering agency.

The language of finance tends to be cold and calculative: risk, return, volatility, efficiency. It is a language engineered for spreadsheets, not psyches. But financial decision-making is inseparably human, marbled with memory, emotion, identity, and—crucially—regret. Regret is not merely retrospective disappointment. It is a distorting force that attaches itself to memory and influences present-day cognition. Studies in behavioural finance consistently show that people do not merely remember losses—they relive them. This reliving reduces the cognitive bandwidth for objective reassessment. *Unforgiven financial regret narrows perception, dulls creative thinking, and can entrench a person in suboptimal behaviours for years.*

One cannot build a clear future with a fogged-up windshield. Owners—those who lead, decide, invest, and take responsibility—require clarity of attention and confidence in judgment. Carrying unprocessed financial regret is like trying to steer with the handbrake partially engaged. To forgive a financial mistake is to reclaim forward momentum.

Forgiveness here is not a moral luxury. It is a strategic imperative. Therapeutic psychology offers essential tools that, when appropriately adapted, can bring profound transformation to financial agency. One of the most foundational practices is the transition from *rumination* to *reflection*. Rumination loops—repetitive negative thought cycles—tend to fixate on perceived personal failure: "I was so stupid," "I should have known," "Everyone else was smarter." Reflection, in contrast, interrogates circumstance and learning: "What data did I have at the time?" "What structural or emotional pressures shaped that decision?" "What patterns have I now outgrown?" The former imprisons, the latter liberates.

Neuroscience underscores this shift. Rumination tends to activate the brain's default mode network, associated with internal narratives and emotional inertia. Reflective thinking, especially when aided by writing or guided prompts, activates prefrontal regions tied to rational analysis, planning, and empathy. *Forgiveness is not forgetfulness—it is emotional integration that restores functional cognition.*

One exercise adapted from therapeutic practice is what clinicians call "double-entry narrative journaling." This involves writing down a regretful financial event in two parallel columns. The left-hand side captures the raw narrative: what happened, what was lost, what was felt. The right-hand column then attempts to annotate that story with compassionate reasoning: what wasn't known at the time, what conditions influenced the decision, what lessons have since been earned. This act externalises the internalised judgment and allows a reader to begin dis-identifying from a static sense of self based on one moment in time.

Consider the example of Anand, a mid-career executive who invested a significant portion of his early savings in a real estate deal with friends that collapsed during a regional market downturn. For years, Anand avoided conversations about investing. He deferred financial planning to his spouse, skipped equity opportunities at work, and ignored mentoring younger colleagues about decision-making—believing himself unworthy of offering financial guidance. It wasn't until a coach invited him to narrate the full timeline of that investment, including his due diligence, the reputational pressure of the group, and the macroeconomic indicators at the time, that he began to see the nuance. He had not failed due to incompetence; he had participated in a complex system with incomplete data. *His mistake had become an identity. Reframing it as a data point returned him to the role of owner.*

Therapeutic literature suggests that regrets, when unprocessed, behave more like trauma than error. They are stored in affective memory, often without clear language, and resurface in avoidance patterns. Financial trauma, unlike physical trauma, often masquerades as pragmatism. The person becomes "cautious," "risk-averse," "conservative." But under those labels lies unexamined fear. Forgiveness is not about becoming reckless—it is about regaining the ability to assess risk without the bias of historical pain.

Financial forgiveness also has implications at the institutional level. Many founders, executives, and even policymakers become locked into strategic positions because acknowledging a past error might be perceived as weakness. But the best leaders are those who treat feedback as an evolving data set. They revise. They pivot. They exit. They narrate their past decisions transparently, signalling not failure, but learning. In doing so, they model *ownership as evolution* rather than perfection.

From a systems perspective, unforgiven regrets act as corrupted code. They introduce bugs into one's decision-making system—biases, blind spots, overcorrections. A person who lost heavily in tech stocks may ignore innovative sectors for a decade, even when valuations and fundamentals have realigned. A founder who exited too early may cling to the next company too long. Without interrupting this cognitive sequence, individuals are not evolving—they are reacting. The discipline of forgiveness breaks this loop. *It allows one to transition from being an emotional captive to a strategic participant.*

There is a productive tension between accountability and forgiveness. Ownership does not mean never making errors; it means metabolising them into better processes. The most effective owners don't avoid mistakes—they transform them. A financial regret, when integrated, becomes an input into a more robust mental model. That is the essence of adaptive thinking. *To forgive is not to excuse; it is to extract learning, archive the event, and move forward unburdened.*

Another practical intervention, this time from Acceptance and Commitment Therapy (ACT), involves the use of "defusion" techniques. When people speak of financial regrets, they often use language like, "I am terrible with money," or "I always make the wrong calls." ACT teaches clients to add a cognitive buffer: "I'm having the thought that I'm terrible with money." This subtle shift creates space between self and narrative. It interrupts the fusion between identity and behaviour. Applied to financial life, this tool lets people observe their inner critic without letting it dictate strategy. *The mind may replay mistakes, but the owner doesn't have to obey those broadcasts.*

There is also an intergenerational dimension to forgiveness. Many individuals carry not only their own regrets, but inherited scripts from parents, mentors, or cultural norms. Messages like "you should never trust the stock market," "debt is always evil," or "wealth corrupts" can become internalised dogma that distorts future action. Forgiving financial regret, then, may also involve interrogating where certain beliefs came from—and whether they still serve the life the individual is building. To forgive a financial past is sometimes to forgive a family system, or at least to rewrite the script with more precision and kindness.

An effective exercise for readers is what therapists call a "timeline of wisdom." Instead of charting net worth, one charts key financial events alongside what was learned, what was feared, what was overcome, and what changed. This timeline becomes a cognitive audit trail—not of wealth, but of growth. When people see their financial life as an evolving story rather than a fixed scorecard, their capacity to act decisively in the present expands.

Ultimately, regret is the tax paid on self-awareness. It signals that one has grown. That new information has become available. That perspective has shifted. But to stay stuck in regret is to freeze at the moment just before the insight matures. Ownership requires completing that maturation cycle. It asks, "What's the next intelligent action now that I know more?" Forgiveness is what lets that question emerge.

To forgive a financial regret is not to rewrite the past—it is to restore agency to the present. That is the terrain of the owner: emotionally clear, strategically engaged, forward-facing. The goal is not to forget what has been lost, but to learn so well from it that the loss transforms into capability. That is how regrets become capital. Not just stories of pain, but resources of wisdom. Not liabilities on an emotional balance sheet, but equity—earned and reinvested.

Joy as a Compass –

There is a quiet power in joy that rarely makes it into financial literature. Excitement, ambition, and urgency dominate the lexicon of investing, entrepreneurship, and wealth creation. Yet, beneath the noise of dopamine-chasing behaviour lies a subtler, more enduring force—joy. Not the fleeting thrill of acquisition or the adrenaline of a market swing, but the kind of grounded, calm contentment that arises when actions and values align. *Joy, when understood as a signal rather than a reward, becomes a compass—not a distraction—guiding individuals towards deeper, long-term financial and life alignment.*

The modern economic system is primed to exploit the neurochemistry of excitement. Digital interfaces deliver rewards in milliseconds; financial markets ping devices with real-time data; social media celebrates hustle culture, conflating activity with achievement. The result is a culture of financial hyperactivity: compulsive trading, over-leveraged bets, or spending driven by insecurity masked as self-care. Yet these behaviours are not random. They are engineered responses to environments optimised for dopamine release—a neurotransmitter that thrives on novelty, risk, and anticipation. This is not inherently bad. But it is not the same thing as joy.

Dopamine-fuelled spending tends to prioritise immediate validation over enduring value. It is the car purchased for status rather than utility, the speculative crypto token bought out of FOMO, the career pivot chosen because everyone else seems to be making one. These decisions often feel electric in the moment, but rarely age well. Excitement has an expiration date. Joy does not.

Joy, by contrast, moves at a slower, quieter frequency. It does not announce itself with fanfare, nor does it require external applause. It often shows up in routine: the peace of a well-balanced ledger, the dignity of financial autonomy, the satisfaction of an investment aligned with personal values. Whereas excitement burns calories, joy conserves energy. It signals that we are acting in accordance with our inner blueprint, rather than reacting to external stimuli.

This distinction has profound implications for financial decision-making. A portfolio constructed around excitement tends to be volatile—not just in terms of asset class, but in the emotional experience of the investor. A portfolio designed with joy as its reference point tends to exhibit both resilience and longevity. It reflects not just what the owner can afford, but what they are proud to own. And this is not abstract sentiment—it has measurable consequences.

Behavioural finance researchers have long noted the impact of emotions on market participation. One longitudinal study by Dalbar, spanning over 20 years, found that the average investor consistently underperformed the market due to emotional decision-making. Buying high in euphoria, selling low in panic. But what if the issue isn't emotion per se, but the *type* of emotion? Joy is not euphoric. It is not manic. It rarely leads to irrational exuberance. Instead, it fosters a level-headed, long-view posture that aligns remarkably well with the requirements of compounding wealth.

Consider the investment ethos of someone like Nick Sleep, a little-known but highly respected investor who ran Nomad Investment Partnership. His strategy was predicated on simplicity, patience, and businesses that created enduring value for customers—rather than hype-fuelled metrics. When asked how he endured periods of underperformance without panicking, his answer was telling: *he enjoyed what he owned.* His investments made him feel calm, not clever. He found joy in integrity, not in outperforming. And the results, over time, were exceptional.

This framework applies far beyond markets. In consumption, too, joy offers a litmus test. Imagine a spending audit not built around shame or guilt, but around *sustained resonance.* What purchases continue to bring satisfaction months—or years—after the receipt faded? Which ones feel hollow in retrospect? When joy is the benchmark, the entire architecture of consumption begins to shift: fewer impulse buys, more investment in durable goods, experiences with compounding emotional returns, relationships over status signalling.

Neuroscience supports this distinction. Dopamine is associated with seeking and anticipation. But joy is more closely tied to serotonin and oxytocin—neurochemicals that reward stability, trust, and emotional connection. These latter systems are quieter, more enduring, and less easily hijacked. They point to the long arc, not the momentary spike.

One powerful way to operationalise this shift is through reflection tools. A simple exercise borrowed from acceptance and commitment therapy (ACT) is the "values ledger." At the end of a week, reflect not on what you earned or bought, but on what brought you sustained meaning. Was your time and money allocated toward things that nourished relationships, built autonomy, cultivated mastery, or promoted wellbeing? Did your choices reflect values or just react to urges?

This practice, when embedded regularly, acts as a kind of emotional P&L statement. It highlights hidden costs—time lost to low-joy activities, money spent on purchases that dulled rather than enriched life. And like any sound accounting practice, it begins to clarify where future investments—of time, capital, and attention—should go.

The tension between joy and excitement becomes especially visible in moments of uncertainty. In volatile markets, excited investors tend to oscillate between fear and greed. Joyful investors, by contrast, often sit still—not out of paralysis, but because they are already where they want to be. This does not mean they ignore data, but rather that they have internal metrics as well as external ones. When values and investments are aligned, decision-making becomes less reactive. And that, over decades, makes an enormous difference.

We see this distinction in entrepreneurial life as well. Entrepreneurs driven by excitement often chase novelty—new markets, new technologies, new rounds of funding. Those oriented toward joy tend to build enduring cultures, nurture employees, and care deeply about legacy. Their decisions are not always faster, but they are often wiser. The companies they build tend to reflect emotional coherence, not just market fit.

One illustrative case is Patagonia under Yvon Chouinard. Rather than chasing scale at all costs, Chouinard repeatedly made decisions that sacrificed short-term excitement for long-term integrity—capping growth, resisting IPO pressure, even donating the entire company to environmental causes. These decisions were not "rational" in the narrow economic sense. But they were deeply rational in a broader, values-aligned frame. *Joy was the compass—and the outcome was not just financial health, but reputational and existential clarity.*

To be clear, joy is not the absence of struggle. It does not immunise one against risk or pain. But it does anchor one's responses. When tough calls must be made—whether to walk away from a job, hold through a drawdown, or say no to a lucrative but misaligned opportunity—joy offers a kind of emotional GPS. It doesn't guarantee ease. But it does preserve direction.

The long-term implications of adopting joy as a decision metric are difficult to overstate. Over time, joy-based systems produce portfolios, careers, and lives that feel *coherent.* They reduce regret not because every choice turns out well, but because each choice *made sense at the time,* given one's values. And that, paradoxically, reduces the emotional cost of losses.

Ultimately, the question is not merely "How much did I earn?" or "How fast did I grow?" but rather, "Was I glad to have owned this, done this, or become this?" Financial alignment without emotional congruence is hollow. Joy is not a soft ideal—it is a critical benchmark of internal consistency.

If wealth is to serve life, then joy must be in the room when decisions are made. Not as a reactive emotion, but as a guiding principle. Not as a luxury, but as a *discipline.* For those thinking like true owners—not merely of assets, but of their attention, time, and choices—joy is not a byproduct. It is the point.

When to Let Go – Explores emotional exits: when to sell, pivot, or walk away

There is a profound silence in the decision to walk away. Not the kind born of failure or cowardice, but one born of discernment—of knowing when continuation would mean decay rather than progress. In wealth building, business, and personal ownership, there's an emotional weight tied to exit decisions. Most of us are taught to glorify endurance, to prize the long-haul, to clutch tightly to things we've spent time and capital building. But holding on indefinitely—whether to a business, an investment, a relationship, or an identity—can erode the very gains we fought to create. Owners who thrive over time are not those who cling indefinitely, but those who learn to *release with reason.*

This subchapter explores one of the most under-discussed, emotionally fraught aspects of financial ownership: the art and timing of letting go. It requires more than logic. It demands introspection, humility, and the ability to sever our sense of self from the narratives we once believed were non-negotiable.

A defining case is Stewart Butterfield, co-founder of Flickr and later, Slack. His success is often romanticised, but what's less discussed is the decision-making agility that allowed him to stop building one product and start another—twice. Both Flickr and Slack emerged from companies that began with completely different missions. The key was Butterfield's ability to spot when the initial vision no longer served reality, and pivot with precision. Letting go of the original idea wasn't a failure of leadership. It was the *expression* of leadership. He exited a vision, not out of desperation, but from clarity. The rewards followed not because he stuck to plan A, but because he knew when it had outlived its usefulness.

Many investors miss this lesson entirely. Take the case of Kodak. It wasn't ignorance that doomed them—they had invented digital photography before it became mainstream. What they lacked was the institutional courage to *let go* of the film-based identity that had defined them for decades. The existential investment was emotional, not just financial. Kodak's leadership didn't fail to see the future; they simply couldn't release the past.

Letting go often feels antithetical to ownership. We associate ownership with accumulation, with legacy, with permanence. But in truth, wise ownership includes the discipline of divestment. This is as true in venture capital as it is in personal finance. Venture capitalists routinely make decisions to shutter underperforming startups. The most successful funds aren't those with the fewest failures—they're the ones that cut losses quickly and reallocate to promising ventures without nostalgia. That requires a framework not built on sunk cost thinking, but on adaptive realism.

Contrast that with the average retail investor who clings to losing stocks, paralysed by the idea of "locking in" a loss. Emotion clouds assessment. What began as an investment becomes a symbol—of competence, of identity, of hope—and symbols are harder to release than numbers. A good owner builds structures for decision-making that make exit less about emotion and more about process. This is where pre-commitment becomes powerful. Having exit criteria defined in advance protects future-you from the emotional distortions of the moment. Think of it as creating a *decision will*—not unlike a living will—articulating what to do under conditions when clarity will be hardest to access.

There's also an emotional dividend to exiting well. Founders who sell companies too early are often critiqued by outsiders for "missing out" on future valuations. But rarely are the intangible gains discussed—mental space, regained time, new creative freedom. Consider the case of Julia Hartz, co-founder of Eventbrite, who consciously paused her operational role after scaling the company to a global platform. She wasn't walking away from ambition—she was walking towards renewal. For thoughtful builders, there's value in knowing that their identity is not wholly anchored to any one venture. Emotional exits are not endings. They're reallocations of agency.

Of course, the opposite trap also exists: quitting too soon. Some use "letting go" as a shield from discomfort, mistaking momentary friction for strategic misalignment. This is where a maturity of discernment is essential. Letting go must not be confused with avoiding adversity. The difference lies in motive and context. Are you exiting because the thing no longer aligns with your deeper values, or because it is momentarily hard? Is this a decision from your highest self—or from fear, fatigue, or frustration?

These are not questions easily answered in spreadsheets. They require a different kind of accounting—a personal *emotional balance sheet* that evaluates not just assets and liabilities, but alignment and dissonance. That includes asking:

> What would I do if I were starting this project or investment *today* with a clean slate?

What am I preserving that no longer serves my future self?

Where does my pride prevent strategic clarity?

These reflective tools, adapted from therapeutic and coaching models, help strip away ego from evaluation. In some practices, such as Acceptance and Commitment Therapy (ACT), letting go is framed not as defeat but as *committed action*—the willingness to drop what's not working in favour of what aligns with values. That's a profound upgrade in mental software. You're not just abandoning a path; you're upgrading the decision system behind the path.

In the context of family wealth, emotional exits take on another dimension. There are families who continue to run businesses for generations—not because they remain optimal, but because tradition has ossified into obligation. One family office in the Netherlands chose to exit its legacy industrial operations after five generations, redirecting capital into sustainability ventures. The choice was met with both internal resistance and eventual clarity: the new investments aligned better with the family's modern values and emerging priorities. Walking away didn't erase heritage—it evolved it.

Equally, financial decisions tied to personal identity—selling a house, leaving a job, closing a business—require the courage to mourn. We often think of mourning as appropriate only for death or loss, but in truth, it applies wherever we have to close a chapter that held emotional significance. One entrepreneur described the experience of shutting down her first company as "a silent grief," not for the money lost, but for the dream that had to be released. What allowed her to move forward was naming that grief, not repressing it. Emotional honesty, not denial, is the lever that enables clean exits.

Ultimately, the best owners recognise that *timing is a skill.* It is not always clear in the moment, but it can be trained through self-awareness, decision audits, and strategic pre-planning. More than grit, more than passion, it's timing that determines whether an exit becomes a platform for reinvention or a trap of regret. And timing is rarely gifted—it must be earned through sustained attentiveness and courageous clarity.

Letting go, then, is not weakness. It is not failure. It is the highest expression of ownership: knowing when what you hold no longer holds you—and acting anyway. The return on such decisions is not always immediate or measurable, but over time, those who master the discipline of graceful exit find themselves richer in both capital and conviction. Because to own well is to know not just what to build, but also when to release—and how to do so with intention, dignity, and design.

Chapter 8
Culture, Legacy, and the Invisible Inheritance

Wealth, despite its ledgers, trusts, and legal codices, is never purely financial. It carries memory, meaning, and the unspoken weight of generations. Behind every portfolio, every estate plan, every trust document, there exist inherited scripts—beliefs, loyalties, wounds, and expectations transmitted quietly across time. These scripts are not always rational, nor consciously chosen. They operate in the background: in family tensions over money, in habitual choices that feel inexplicable, in stories about who deserves what, and in silences that speak louder than any will.

This chapter turns attention to culture, legacy, and what might be called the invisible inheritance—the forces that shape financial behaviour before a single coin has changed hands. While traditional finance education emphasises accumulation and preservation of capital, far less is devoted to the emotional scaffolding on which wealth rests—or collapses. A family may amass substantial assets yet lose trust along the way. An individual may grow a considerable net worth while unconsciously replaying the scarcity scripts of their youth. Even well-intentioned parents can pass on wealth while embedding conflict, failing to convey meaning. These dynamics are structural, not anecdotal.

Consider inherited scripts. Psychologists and family systems theorists have long observed that individuals unconsciously adopt roles, loyalties, and beliefs from previous generations. A father who never saves may be echoing a parent who regarded money with shame. A daughter who overworks may carry the silent burden of a grandfather's failure. These narratives are not always consciously embraced, yet they often guide behaviour—especially around money. One effective tool in family therapy and intergenerational wealth work is the genogram: a visual map of family patterns across generations. Applied to financial behaviour—risk tolerance, giving patterns, investment strategies, attitudes toward debt—a genogram can illuminate stories that influence choices far more than market data ever could.

Family offices increasingly enlist psychologists, anthropologists, and narrative coaches to help heirs understand not merely what they are inheriting, but why it matters. In one well-documented case, a third-generation wealth holder resisted assuming leadership in the family philanthropic trust. Superficially, this appeared as apathy. Guided narrative work revealed a deep, unconscious loyalty to his grandfather, a self-made industrialist who had declared, "I don't believe in handouts." Though the grandson intellectually endorsed the foundation's mission, he emotionally equated philanthropy with betrayal. Once that script was surfaced, it could be reframed—edited without being erased.

The broader lesson is clear: we inherit more than assets; we inherit meaning systems. Left unexamined, these systems dictate behaviour under the illusion of rationality.

Legacy, too, requires reframing—not as a static object awaiting bequest, but as a living practice that begins now. Conventional thinking often postpones legacy until estate planning, treating values transmission as a ceremonial afterthought. Yet enduring legacies are enacted, embodied, and witnessed. Some families integrate storytelling into their wealth architecture. One foundation in New Zealand hosts intergenerational storytelling retreats, where members share personal money memories—painful and proud alike. These narratives have been codified into family values, guiding strategic choices in grants and investments. Legacy, in this model, is not posthumous; it is visible in decisions made today.

This perspective profoundly affects succession planning. Research shows family enterprises rarely fail solely due to economic pressures. Breakdowns usually stem from misaligned values, communication failures, or identity conflicts. These are not financial issues—they are narrative issues. The remedy is meaning-making. Ownership, particularly across generations, demands shared purpose. Without it, structures are brittle; with it, they gain resilience no market downturn can shake.

Financial trauma must also be confronted—especially in families or communities shaped by colonisation, displacement, or generational scarcity. Such trauma is rarely individual; it can be cultural, collective, even epigenetic. Consider the "money silence" often observed in immigrant households: money is central yet secret, survival and pride entwined with shame. The next generation may inherit hyper-vigilance, over-saving tendencies, or burnout.

Healing this legacy is essential. Financial planners and coaches increasingly incorporate trauma-informed approaches, recognising that strategies must be paired with emotional repair. Exercises adapted from therapeutic practice—writing "letters of financial forgiveness" to ancestors or reenacting ancestral money conversations—allow individuals to move from inherited scripts to consciously authored ones, from unconscious repetition to intentional design.

The conversation cannot stop at the individual. Institutional structures also shape which legacies are rewarded or erased. Western financial models emphasise individual accumulation, linear growth, and private ownership. By contrast, many Indigenous cultures prioritise stewardship, cyclical time, and interdependence. When these frameworks intersect—especially in estate planning, land rights, or entrepreneurship—the dominant model often assumes neutrality. It is not neutral. True legacy work recognises and makes space for alternative cultural logics.

Consider Māori collective land trusts in Aotearoa New Zealand, where governance involves elders, youth, and cultural custodians, and economic decisions are filtered through spiritual and ecological lenses. Or matrilineal inheritance in parts of Ghana, where property passes through the mother's line—a structure challenging Western assumptions about capital flow. These examples remind us that legacy is not simply what we pass on, but how we frame wealth's meaning.

This chapter also invites readers to locate themselves within this ecosystem. You may not come from a visibly wealthy family, yet you have inherited narratives—about money's meaning, its accessibility, and its moral weight. Some beliefs serve you; others constrain.

Perhaps austerity taught discipline but suppressed joy. Perhaps abundance offered access but obscured accountability. Intentional ownership begins with excavating these foundations—not discarding them wholesale, but choosing consciously which parts to preserve, question, or evolve.

Ultimately, the invisible inheritance is not a burden—it is a blueprint. Made visible, it becomes a canvas for design. Through storytelling, structured reflection, and redesigned governance, one can author legacy in real time. The aim is not merely to transfer assets, but to cultivate continuity of purpose. Culture and capital are inseparable, braided together. And it is through that braid—part bloodline, part intention, part repair—that the most enduring legacies endure.

Inherited Scripts, Unconscious Loyalties –

Most people assume their financial behaviour stems from personal choice, informed analysis, or formal education. But beneath conscious decision-making lies an inherited psychological code—one passed down silently through family culture, generational trauma, and unspoken loyalties. These inherited financial scripts often predate our understanding of money itself. They shape what we feel we're entitled to, what we fear, how we invest, how we give, and even how we interpret risk and security.

This is not metaphorical. Decades of clinical family systems work, particularly from the fields of genogram analysis, systemic therapy, and transgenerational coaching, have made it clear: *family narratives around money are encoded in behaviour long before they are articulated in words.* When those narratives go unexamined, they can unconsciously override logic, opportunity, or technical financial literacy.

Consider a common pattern in family offices: the second-generation inheritor who, despite receiving a robust financial education, cannot bring themselves to take calculated investment risks. Upon deeper examination, what emerges is a loyalty to a grandparent who survived wartime scarcity. That ancestor may have taught—implicitly or explicitly—that survival comes from hoarding, not risk-taking. The grandchild, acting from inherited allegiance rather than insight, avoids decisions that could benefit them or the enterprise. This is not personal dysfunction; it's systemically inherited programming.

Family genograms offer one of the most effective tools for surfacing these hidden dynamics. A genogram is a family diagram that maps relationships, patterns, roles, and emotional intensities across three or more generations. Originally developed for therapeutic use, genograms are now increasingly employed by wealth advisors and legacy consultants to make visible what remains unsaid: the invisible loyalties that shape financial habits.

One prominent example involves a European family office that began experiencing stagnation across its entrepreneurial portfolio. A new generation of leaders appeared reluctant to lead, citing burnout, over-caution, or lack of clarity. A systemic consultant introduced genogram analysis. It revealed an intergenerational story of family members burning out or dying prematurely after gaining control of the family business. The younger leaders, unconsciously loyal to those lost, were 'choosing' professional mediocrity as a way to stay alive and emotionally connected. Once this script was revealed and processed, several family members took bold yet emotionally grounded steps—delegating authority, redesigning roles, and launching philanthropic ventures that aligned more honestly with their personal values.

Unconscious loyalty is rarely about money on the surface—but it exerts enormous influence over money in practice. We may unconsciously replicate a parent's sabotage of abundance, a grandparent's belief that money is shameful, or a sibling's assumption that wealth causes disconnection. In systemic terms, what we do not reconcile, we often re-enact. Breaking free from these cycles requires more than insight—it demands a deep reframing of what loyalty, belonging, and integrity mean within the context of financial life.

This work is not simply psychological introspection. The implications are strategic. In a study conducted by Cambridge Institute for Family Enterprise, families that integrate psychological systems thinking into their financial governance are significantly more likely to sustain wealth beyond the third generation. This is not because they have better investment strategies, but because they understand the invisible architecture driving decision-making within the family itself.

This explains why some of the most sophisticated family offices have begun to treat genogram mapping as essential—not optional—in succession planning and governance design. It is not enough to teach heirs how to manage capital. One must also illuminate the ancestral narratives they may be unconsciously obeying. These narratives often involve survival logic: fear of loss, guilt over privilege, or inherited martyrdom. *Until named and examined, these drivers will quietly undermine even the most technically sound financial decisions.*

The concept of "invisible inheritance" reframes wealth as something far more complex than assets on a balance sheet. We inherit stories, roles, loyalties, beliefs about deservingness, and moral codes about how money should or shouldn't be used. In some cases, the most powerful inheritance is a wound—carried forward until it is either healed or passed on again. This invisible inheritance is rarely discussed in formal financial planning, yet it drives everything from investment posture to philanthropic impulse.

One of the most powerful questions an individual can ask when reviewing a financial decision is: *Who might I be unconsciously trying to remain loyal to?* The answer is rarely straightforward—but consistently illuminating. Sometimes it is a parent who believed that wealth isolates. Sometimes it is a cultural script suggesting that security is inherently fragile and must be over-controlled. Sometimes it is a sibling who suffered through financial failure and whose emotional proximity makes personal success feel like betrayal.

Case study after case study reveals a sobering insight: *Financial underperformance is often emotionally rational.* That is, what appears irrational or self-defeating in market terms often makes perfect sense as an expression of inherited identity, guilt, grief, or unconscious loyalty. The solution is not to shame or 'fix' the behaviour, but to bring it to light and integrate it consciously into a broader, healthier identity.

This is especially relevant in post-exit transitions—when founders sell companies, inheritances are transferred, or trusts are activated. Many individuals experience sudden surges of anxiety, self-sabotage, or decision paralysis during these times. It's tempting to attribute this to poor planning. More often, it is the surfacing of unresolved scripts: what does it mean to be someone who no longer "earns"? What role must I now play? What loyalties am I honouring—or betraying—by spending, investing, or giving?

The technical infrastructure of wealth must be complemented by the emotional architecture of understanding. Without both, families risk building empires on invisible fractures. Legacy advisors are increasingly trained to recognise these fault lines—not just for risk mitigation, but to cultivate alignment, integrity, and wellbeing. Money is never just about money. It is a carrier of values, memory, trauma, and love.

Practitioners working with families—whether in legal, financial, or governance capacities—must develop literacy in systemic dynamics. It is no longer acceptable to focus solely on performance metrics while ignoring the emotional engines beneath them. Understanding inherited scripts is not a fringe exercise; it is central to ensuring long-term financial sustainability, relational cohesion, and clarity of purpose.

For readers, the invitation is both analytical and deeply personal. Examine not only your cashflow, but your conditioning. Audit not only your portfolio, but your internal programming. Consider the stories your family told—or refused to tell—about wealth, success, scarcity, and responsibility. Draw your own genogram. Interview your elders. Ask what money meant to them, and what it cost.

This is not merely therapeutic work. It is strategic stewardship. As families seek to transition wealth across generations without eroding trust or cohesion, it becomes clear that *clarity is not a product of spreadsheets alone.* It is born of self-awareness, courageous conversation, and the willingness to confront what has remained emotionally unspoken.

True ownership begins where unconscious loyalty ends. And legacy begins—not with what you leave behind—but with what you choose to see clearly now.

Transmitting Values, Not Just Assets –

Wealth preserved without meaning tends to dissipate. This is not a moral axiom; it is a practical observation echoed by family offices, behavioural economists, and seasoned advisors across generations. When families treat money as an isolated asset—divorced from identity, purpose, and the values that shaped its creation—it becomes fragile, directionless, and eventually corrosive. The most enduring wealth legacies are not engineered through superior investment strategy alone. They are sustained through intentional transmission of values—narratives, behaviours, and shared moral reference points that create coherence across time. What is often misunderstood as a "dynasty" is, at its most functional, a system of meaning-making. Families that last don't just pass down capital; they pass down the compass by which to use it.

The question, then, is not simply how to distribute assets, but how to encode them with purpose. And that requires language. It requires story. It requires frameworks that allow the next generation to ask: *What was this money for? Who were we before we had it? What does responsibility look like now that we do?*

At the core of this challenge is the reality that values are not inherited passively. They are not received through osmosis or dictated through estate plans. They are transmitted through repeated exposure, emotional imprinting, and—critically—intentional conversation. Families who assume that their heirs will "just know" what matters most often find, decades later, that those values have been replaced by abstraction, anxiety, or entitlement. By contrast, families who proactively cultivate value-alignment treat this as a craft: deliberate, iterative, and shaped by the recognition that what is emotionally unspoken is financially unstable.

One of the most powerful illustrations of this principle comes from a three-generation family based in the Netherlands, whose family office oversees both a legacy manufacturing enterprise and a philanthropic trust. During a leadership retreat, a second-generation heir openly admitted that for years she had resisted taking a seat on the family board—not out of disinterest, but out of fear that she didn't understand what her father's legacy was really *for*. His directives were impeccably clear, his spreadsheets perfectly updated, but his *intentions* had never been verbalised. In his silence, she had constructed a narrative: that he only valued operational efficiency, that there was no room for risk, that her background in sustainable design would be irrelevant. When, during a facilitated session, he revealed that his original ambition had been to create "an enterprise that could employ the sons and daughters of war refugees"—the room fell quiet. The tone of the discussion changed permanently. That story reframed the balance sheet.

This is not sentimentalism. It is governance. *Values transmission is not an emotional luxury—it is a structural necessity for sustainable ownership.*

Consider the role of storytelling as a tool of economic education. In family wealth contexts, stories function as memory architecture. They serve to locate individual actors within a shared lineage—highlighting not only the victories of forebears, but their vulnerabilities, dilemmas, and evolving philosophies. The most enduring families have a narrative infrastructure: they don't just know *what* great-grandfather did; they know *why* he made the choices he did, what values he upheld, where he failed, and how the family adapted. This historical literacy doesn't emerge automatically—it is cultivated through rituals of retelling, intergenerational dialogue, and, crucially, open curiosity.

One prominent model for facilitating this process is the "values alignment interview," now widely employed by legacy consultants and multi-family offices. In this model, family members—often across three generations—are each invited to articulate what they believe the family stands for. These responses are not judged or ranked. Instead, they are mapped side by side to reveal themes, tensions, and blind spots. Often, younger members surface insights older members had forgotten: "We give generously, but we never talk about why." Or: "Grandmother made every major decision around education. But we never discuss learning as a core family value." These conversations surface the implicit codes that govern financial decision-making. When made explicit, these codes can be refined, updated, and embodied with new energy.

In practical terms, values need mechanisms. One of the most elegant is the use of "legacy letters"—first-person narratives composed by elder members not to dictate terms, but to offer philosophical grounding. These letters are not legal documents. They are personal reflections on how wealth came to be, what its purpose is, and what kind of character the writer hopes future generations will develop. Many families incorporate these into annual retreats, sometimes reading a new letter aloud as part of an opening ceremony. Others embed such letters into the preamble of family constitutions or as annotations to trust documents. The common thread: values must be documented in human terms, not merely financial language.

Still, storytelling is not enough. It must be linked to *structures*. Consider the example of a South African entrepreneur whose family foundation includes a "reverse grant" system. Each year, the youngest adult member is invited to present a cause or issue they care about. The foundation matches their proposed contribution tenfold—on the condition that they report back with outcomes, emotional reflections, and lessons learned. The initiative serves two purposes: it introduces philanthropic discipline and surfaces emerging values. In one such instance, a 21-year-old daughter chose to fund a mental health programme for adolescent boys, citing the silence she'd witnessed around emotional trauma in her boarding school. Her report became the seed of a new core theme for the family: "psychological well-being as economic infrastructure." That phrase is now etched into the foundation's guiding principles.

What is clear across case studies like these is that values transmission cannot be outsourced. Financial advisors can scaffold the process, consultants can prompt dialogue, but ultimately the work must be relational. This means accepting messiness. Families must tolerate ambiguity, welcome divergent views, and navigate the discomfort that comes from surfacing misalignments. Wealth, when paired with suppressed conflict, becomes brittle. But when paired with transparent, values-driven conversation, it becomes a dynamic platform for growth.

Critically, the aim is not uniformity. It is coherence. A high-functioning family enterprise does not require identical political beliefs, investment styles, or life philosophies. What it does require is a *shared language* for evaluating decisions—particularly in moments of uncertainty. A family who agrees, for instance, that "we value entrepreneurial boldness over preservationism" will make different succession choices than one that prioritises caution and conservatism. The key is not which value is selected—but that the selection is conscious, articulated, and trusted across the generational spectrum.

This becomes particularly vital during transitions of control. Studies consistently show that most intergenerational wealth transfers fail not because of taxation, poor investment, or market loss, but because of *breakdowns in communication and trust.* Values, when not transmitted, leave heirs disoriented. When transmitted poorly—through platitudes, secrecy, or control—they leave heirs resentful. But when done with clarity, empathy, and context, they provide the single most resilient foundation a family can offer: *a compass, not just a map.*

Some of the most effective tools here borrow from therapeutic practice. Family constellations, guided narrative therapy, and structured roleplay exercises have been adapted by forward-thinking legacy practitioners to bring submerged dynamics into light. These are not abstract theories. They are interventions rooted in the lived reality of financial stewardship under emotional complexity.

A final note worth emphasising: values evolve. The family that built its wealth through steel may now be investing in renewables. The patriarch who once dismissed philanthropy may have descendants building social enterprises. A family culture grounded in post-war frugality may now be reckoning with excess. These shifts are not failures of loyalty—they are evidence of adaptation. The role of the elder is not to freeze meaning, but to frame it. To offer enough scaffolding that the next generation can build forward, not just look back.

To transmit values is to trust that the future will ask new questions—but will do so with the right principles at hand. Families who master this craft do not simply preserve wealth. They animate it. And in doing so, they extend the meaning of ownership beyond assets—into identity, integrity, and ongoing collective authorship.

Legacy as Living Practice –

Legacy is often spoken of in terms of death—a solemn summary delivered after the subject has already exited the stage. Obituaries, foundations, and endowments all play a part in this narrative. But this traditional framing misses the deeper, more consequential truth: *legacy is not what you leave behind; it is what you live into every day.* The most enduring legacies are not measured in monuments, plaques, or trusts but in patterns of behaviour, decisions that echo, and values that reshape the environments they touch. To treat legacy as a matter for posthumous consideration is to abdicate one's most powerful opportunity to influence the world while still alive.

To live as if legacy begins now is to shift the locus of meaning from memory to momentum. It invites individuals to ask not just "What will they say about me when I'm gone?" but "What do my actions say now, when I can still course-correct, deepen, and demonstrate?" This perspective requires an integration of long-term thinking with present-day integrity—a form of behavioural alignment that many people find more difficult than financial planning itself. It is easy to defer meaning to the end. It is harder, and infinitely more important, to practise it in the messy, incremental flow of ordinary life.

Modern behavioural science backs this reframing. Studies in narrative psychology show that people derive identity not from isolated achievements but from coherent stories they author about themselves over time. Living legacy, then, is about authorship—choosing and revising the storyline through present action rather than posthumous revisionism. Similarly, research from family systems theory underscores that multigenerational impact is not solely determined by net worth but by *relational modelling*: how elders handle conflict, pursue purpose, and embody values in visible, teachable ways. Legacy transmitted through example is far stickier than that transmitted through instruction.

This has significant implications for those managing wealth, influence, or leadership roles. Too often, legacy planning is confined to legal instruments and asset allocations. While essential, these technical tools are structurally insufficient. They tell beneficiaries what they will receive but not *why* they received it. They create permanence without context. To build a living legacy, the owner must be present—not just physically alive, but philosophically engaged. The questions shift: What am I modelling? What norms am I reinforcing? Who is watching me and learning silently? These are not rhetorical inquiries; they are architectural.

Consider the example of Anita Chauhan, a second-generation tech entrepreneur in London whose family built wealth through property in the 1980s. Rather than waiting to pass on assets through inheritance, Anita has integrated her two teenage children into active philanthropic decision-making, offering them real stakes in the causes the family supports. Monthly, they meet to review donation outcomes, meet grantees, and reflect on impact. While the capital itself may be modest, the effect on her children's understanding of stewardship, empathy, and agency is profound. As Anita puts it, "We're not giving money; we're training hands."

This principle also applies in organisational contexts. Founders and CEOs often imagine their legacy as tied to their exit—IPO, sale, or succession. But leadership literature increasingly demonstrates that cultural imprint is most durable when consciously embedded into daily operations, long before departure. Herb Kelleher of Southwest Airlines, for instance, didn't just write values on the wall; he embodied them—visiting staff on holidays, answering customer complaints personally, and treating humour not as garnish but as operational ethos. By living his legacy, he multiplied its durability. Even years after his passing, employees still cite "what Herb would've done" as a behavioural litmus test.

There's a common objection: "I'm too early in my career/life/wealth journey to think about legacy." But this assumes that legacy begins when one reaches a certain threshold—of success, of age, of social standing. This is a false premise. *Every financial decision is a cultural decision.* Every allocation of time, energy, or capital either reinforces or revises the story we are telling about who we are and what matters.

Waiting until some imagined milestone to begin 'legacy work' is like deciding to start exercising only once you're already fit. Legacy is cumulative, not ceremonial.

This shift in orientation—from future-centric to present-enacted legacy—also introduces a new set of tools and strategies. One such tool is the "visible values ledger," a practice where individuals track not just their net worth but the instances in which their values were made concrete through action. Did I honour a commitment that was inconvenient? Did I speak truth when it was costly? Did I align my spending this week with my stated priorities? Over time, such tracking creates a parallel record of integrity—one far more instructive than a list of accomplishments.

Another approach is what behavioural designers call *embedded signalling*. This involves structuring routines, rituals, and systems so that values are not just aspirational but architectural. For example, a family that values environmental responsibility might embed carbon impact review into its investment committee meetings. Or an executive who values equity might refuse to approve any hiring shortlist that lacks demographic diversity. These are not symbolic gestures—they are infrastructural commitments. They make the value operational, not ornamental.

The concept of a living legacy also demands a confrontation with ego. To live one's legacy requires relinquishing some control over how one will be remembered, in favour of greater influence over how one is currently perceived and experienced. It prioritises integrity over image, substance over story. It also requires a willingness to evolve. A legacy that is actively lived must, by definition, be capable of revision. That is not a threat to its strength—it is a testament to its vitality. As values deepen, change, or expand, so too can the ways in which they are demonstrated.

Importantly, this is not merely a personal practice. It has profound communal and intergenerational consequences. When individuals begin living their values publicly and consistently, they create what sociologists call "cultural transmission mechanisms"—habits, stories, and examples that others absorb, often unconsciously. A father who discusses investment setbacks with emotional honesty teaches his children more about resilience than any trust document could. A business owner who walks away from a profitable deal on ethical grounds creates folklore inside the company that will likely outlive any formal ethics policy.

Wealth, power, and influence all magnify the reach of this cultural contagion. Which is why those in positions of ownership must consider not just what they will distribute, but what they are already diffusing. The stakes are not abstract. In family offices around the world, practitioners are seeing an increasing divide between those who treat legacy as a static inheritance and those who treat it as a dynamic practice. The former often suffer from entitlement, fragmentation, and philosophical drift. The latter demonstrate cohesion, adaptability, and a rare kind of moral confidence. Not because they have scripted the future, but because they have lived the script now.

This reframing of legacy is not sentimental. It is strategic. It offers a way to use one's most renewable resource—daily behaviour—to shape outcomes that are otherwise left to chance or estate law. It places emphasis where it belongs: not on what we leave behind, but on what we build into the lives of others while we still can.

To live legacy is to close the distance between principle and practice. It is to say: I will not wait for my eulogy to express what I stand for. I will show you now. I will prove it in policy, in posture, in pattern. I will not hope that the next generation understands—I will make sure they can see it, ask about it, challenge it, and continue it. Because the most powerful legacies do not begin at death. *They begin the moment we decide to live deliberately.*

Cultural Money Wounds –

We rarely discuss money in emotional terms, let alone in cultural ones. Yet for millions of people shaped by colonisation, migration, enslavement, exile, or systemic discrimination, the relationship to wealth is anything but neutral. Embedded in daily decisions about earning, saving, giving, or investing are the unspoken residues of cultural trauma—stories of lack, fear, distrust, and survival that live not just in memory, but in behaviour. These are not merely psychological quirks. They are *cultural money wounds*: deeply embedded patterns formed in response to historical disruption and passed across generations, often unconsciously.

To treat wealth as purely rational is to ignore the emotional legacies embedded within it. Many individuals from marginalised or formerly colonised communities experience money not simply as a tool, but as a site of historical grief. For descendants of enslaved people, money may carry the unbearable echo of commodification. For children of war refugees, frugality may masquerade as prudence but stem from a lineage of dispossession. For indigenous families, wealth accumulation may be fraught with the memory of stolen lands and lost sovereignty. In each case, financial behaviour is not just about economics—it's about identity, belonging, and survival.

This framing challenges the conventional assumption that financial literacy alone can close wealth gaps or heal dysfunction. Literacy without cultural insight risks becoming another form of erasure. When financial education ignores emotional and historical context, it reinforces a damaging myth: that individuals simply need to make better choices. In truth, many are already doing their best *within the limits of inherited scripts*. Healing requires more than information—it requires integration.

One cannot overstate the intergenerational dimension of these wounds. Family narratives around money are often internalised before a child can count. Consider the child who watches her parents pay for groceries in cash because "banks can't be trusted"—a belief rooted not in paranoia but in real histories of institutional exclusion. Or the immigrant father who tells his son, "We don't talk about money outside the house," because previous generations were surveilled, taxed unfairly, or punished for perceived wealth. These scripts aren't accidental; they are survival technologies. But what once protected may now limit.

Family systems therapy has long recognised that trauma transmits through unexamined loyalty—often showing up as patterned behaviour that feels moral or instinctual. In financial terms, this might manifest as guilt over financial success, reluctance to invest, an inability to receive help, or compulsive overgiving. These expressions are not irrational. They are evidence of unconscious allegiance to the pain of previous generations. As family therapist Dr. Monica McGoldrick explains, "What the family does not talk about, the child acts out." Without intentional reflection, descendants live out the emotional legacies of their lineage rather than evolving them.

Family offices working with multicultural clients are increasingly turning to tools like the *genogram*—a visual map of familial and relational patterns—to illuminate how economic behaviours track across generations. A genogram allows individuals to surface connections between major life events (migration, bankruptcy, early death, land loss) and inherited financial attitudes. For example, one client, a third-generation South Asian woman managing her parents' estate, discovered through this mapping that her grandmother's dowry had been liquidated to escape Partition violence. Her aversion to long-term planning was not a personal shortcoming; it was an echo. Awareness did not erase the impact, but it made it comprehensible—and therefore transformable.

Healing cultural money wounds is not about abandoning tradition or rejecting ancestors. It is about *choosing which parts of our inheritance we continue, and which we revise.* That discernment requires spaciousness—emotional, relational, and cognitive. Without that space, inherited fear or guilt can dominate financial decisions, even among high-net-worth individuals. The wealthier someone becomes, the more emotionally complicated their relationship with their cultural identity can grow. Do they feel they have betrayed their roots? Are they now the object of suspicion from within their community? These are not abstract concerns—they are daily realities for many.

Part of the work, then, is restoring trust in one's own agency without disavowing the struggle that came before. One useful exercise in this process is the *money timeline reflection*. Individuals are invited to list the major financial events or messages from each decade of their life—and, when known, the lives of their parents and grandparents. What emerges is often startling: moments of loss, sacrifice, or shame that explain present-day triggers. This process doesn't just generate self-awareness; it gives the adult self permission to reframe, rather than react.

Another approach is what some therapists call *emotional budgeting*. Just as one might allocate pounds or euros, clients are encouraged to allocate time and attention to core emotional needs that intersect with money: safety, dignity, expression, generosity, independence. For a client whose family history included forced migration, spending money on beauty or art might initially trigger shame—"This is frivolous." But when reframed as reclaiming aesthetic agency, the act becomes both personal and political. *Spending can be a form of healing—if it's intentional and emotionally coherent.*

Some wounds also manifest collectively. Communities historically denied access to capital often develop what scholar Shawn Ginwright calls "collective trauma"—a shared sense of injustice that shapes group norms. This can surface as community pressure not to appear "too rich," or as resistance to institutions that promise financial mobility. Without naming this dynamic, even well-designed development efforts may fail. For example, microloan programmes in postcolonial regions have floundered not because of poor economics but because they triggered memories of debt-based colonial control. Healing, in such cases, must be *co-created*, not imposed.

There is also a spiritual dimension to this healing. Many traditional cultures view wealth not as private property but as *relational energy*—something to be circulated, not hoarded. Restoring ancestral perspectives on money can serve as a corrective to hyper-individualistic models of wealth. For instance, in Māori communities in Aotearoa (New Zealand), intergenerational land stewardship is increasingly being reasserted as a counterweight to extractive capitalism. This is not regression—it is adaptation. It reminds us that the healthiest financial systems are those that honour *history, context, and community* alongside profit.

Professionals in finance, therapy, and education can support this healing by moving beyond generic advice and towards what writer Resmaa Menakem calls *somatic abolitionism*—recognising how trauma lives in the body and must be addressed through more than intellect.

This includes using nonverbal methods like storytelling, ritual, and movement in financial coaching sessions. It includes making space for silence, ambiguity, and tears—recognising that money is rarely just about money. And it includes asking better questions: not "What are your financial goals?" but "What did your family learn was safe or dangerous about wealth?"

To do this work well requires cultural humility. Advisors and professionals must be willing to hold complexity without simplifying or pathologising. They must understand that trust may be slow to build and easily lost. But the reward is profound. When individuals begin to name and tend to their cultural money wounds, they unlock a different kind of wealth—one rooted not only in financial capital but in *emotional coherence, cultural integrity, and intergenerational clarity.*

This is the invisible repair work that must accompany visible economic change. It is the difference between accumulating wealth and *embodying well-being.* It is not soft—it is strategic. And it is no longer optional. As global wealth flows increasingly intersect with histories of harm, this kind of work will define the future of inclusive, ethical prosperity. The wounds are real. But so is the power to heal—and to write a new script.

Chapter 9
Sovereignty

Success, as commonly measured, has an uncanny uniformity. Titles, income, influence, the sheer scale of achievement—these are the coordinates modern societies tend to fixate upon. Yet beneath this polished veneer lies a subtler disquiet: many high-achieving individuals feel strangely dispossessed of themselves. They climb ladders propped against the wrong walls, optimising for efficiency while outsourcing the authorship of their own lives. What is absent is not merely rest or meaning. It is sovereignty—the capacity to govern one's own life, decisions, and definitions.

This chapter opens with a provocation: what if true wealth is not accumulation, but autonomy? What if the ultimate dividend of financial success is not more consumption, but more discretion—over how time is spent, who one answers to, what one builds, and what one chooses to relinquish? Sovereignty reframes ownership at its apex. It is not simply holding assets; it is holding discretion. It is the power to act without distortion, think without fear, and live in harmony with core values—even when markets, industries, or cultures press in otherwise.

Redefining success is not a philosophical indulgence; it is an economic act. Values and valuations are entwined. When success is externally defined, individuals compromise compulsively to achieve it. Visibility is pursued at the expense of privacy, scale at the expense of integrity, capital at the expense of conviction. Anchor success internally, however, and a different set of trade-offs arises. One might choose a smaller enterprise to protect intellectual freedom, a slower growth trajectory to preserve relationships, or a less prestigious position to safeguard creative control. These are not sacrifices—they are strategies when sovereignty, not appearance, is the measure.

Consider the disciplined contrarian investor—not the caricature of risk for its own sake, but the principled thinker who acts according to enduring values, even at social or financial cost. Anne Wojcicki, co-founder of 23andMe, declined high-profile partnerships early on because they conflicted with her vision of accessible, individual health data. Yvon Chouinard, founder of Patagonia, built an empire on the conviction that environmental stewardship belongs in business models, not just corporate social responsibility reports. Their convictions were operational, not ornamental; when applied intelligently, conviction becomes a form of compounding capital.

Sovereignty does not demand wealth, but it does require design. The concept of decentralised life design draws from systems thinking, minimalism, and antifragility. It encourages constructing lives less dependent on brittle institutions and more responsive to personal truths. Those who live on less may not be retreating from ambition—they may be purchasing freedom from lifestyle inflation. Those who cultivate multiple income streams are not merely hedging risk—they are reclaiming the right to exit. Decentralisation in life design is as much psychological as technical; it nurtures resilience by refusing to tether wellbeing to a single node of approval, income, or identity.

Deep subtraction is part of this work. Sovereignty is often less about adding frameworks and more about removing inherited scripts—what one "should" do, who one "should" become, how one "should" spend. Without pruning, life becomes a patchwork of others' expectations. Harry Frankfurt distinguished between first-order desires (what we want) and second-order volitions (what we want to want). Sovereign individuals operate from the latter: they are not passive consumers of external appetites but authors of their own. This self-authorship is not narcissism; it is responsibility, for one cannot steward what one has not claimed.

Financial independence is only part of the picture. Many financially secure people remain emotionally tethered to validation, addicted to comparison, or paralysed by indecision. Sovereignty must therefore be psychological. It entails the capacity to say no without guilt, change course without collapse, and hold values through volatility. Developmental psychology frames this as adult ego development at its zenith: a shift from reactive behaviour to self-authoring, and ultimately to self-transforming mental structures.

Sovereignty is not isolation. It does not require atomisation. Rather, it entails choosing relationships instead of inheriting them by obligation; collaborating out of alignment, not coercion; and participating in communities structured around mutual aid rather than performance. True sovereignty is interdependence—neither dependency nor detachment, but the freedom to engage and exit on principled terms. It is not monastic withdrawal but intentional participation.

The chapter concludes with the idea of becoming the trustee of one's own life, borrowed from estate law but applied inwardly. A trustee does not own the trust; they manage it according to the grantor's intent. Positioning oneself as trustee of one's existence encourages viewing time, energy, talent, and values as sacred trusts. Decisions are made for long-term congruence, not immediate comfort. Asking, "If I were managing this life for someone I loved, how would I steward it?" often yields clarity sharper than any ambition alone.

What emerges is a multidimensional conception of sovereignty: not detachment, but discernment; not control, but clarity; not rejection of ambition, but a mature negotiation with it. Sovereignty does not promise ease, but it delivers integrity. In a world where noise is cheap and alignment scarce, integrity itself becomes an asset class.

Ownership at its highest octave is revealed here: not mere accumulation, but the deliberate deployment of agency; not the worship of independence, but the craft of interdependent design; not the pursuit of success, but the authorship of it. To live sovereignly is not to reject the world, but to engage with it from a place of anchored, thoughtful presence. That, ultimately, is the enduring essence of freedom.

Redefining Success –

For most of modern history, success has been defined by proximity to power, accumulation of capital, and external markers of status. It's a definition inherited, not questioned—deeply rooted in industrial values, colonial hierarchies, and the psychology of scarcity. It is no accident that the most revered symbols of success—

prestigious job titles, luxury goods, follower counts, investment returns—are all externally visible, easily benchmarked, and often anxiety-inducing. Yet as the cultural velocity of ambition increases, so does a quiet disillusionment. Individuals achieve more than previous generations dared to dream, and still feel strangely misaligned. The scoreboard says they're winning, but the inner signal is flat. The problem is not lack of success. It's a failure to *interrogate its definition.*

To redefine success in any meaningful way requires more than semantics. It demands a dismantling of inherited scripts. Most people pursue success with a borrowed map—chasing goals that were never truly their own, responding to pressures shaped by others' needs, not their own sense of wholeness. Psychologist Carl Rogers spoke of "conditions of worth"—the implicit expectations we absorb early in life about what makes us valuable. These conditions often shape financial aspirations more powerfully than raw ambition or logic. The executive who obsessively chases net worth may be replaying childhood scripts about safety. The creative who self-sabotages may be navigating an invisible loyalty to parents who feared success. What we call "drive" is often unresolved narrative.

This is why redefining success begins with self-authorship. The first and hardest task is to ask: *What do I actually want?* Not what is impressive, not what is safe, not what will silence my critics—but what feels aligned with the deeper rhythm of my life. This is not an indulgent question. It is a strategic one. Because only when success is internally anchored can it become sustainable. Without that anchor, success becomes performative—a treadmill of effort directed outward but disconnected inward. The risk isn't just burnout. It's misalignment: winning a game that no longer matters to you.

In contrast, defining success on one's own terms introduces a new framework—one that integrates financial independence with psychological freedom. These two are not always correlated. Some individuals reach financial autonomy yet remain imprisoned by guilt, fear, or chronic comparison. Others earn modestly but experience profound spaciousness and joy because they've detached self-worth from external metrics. The distinction is not income—it's agency. *True success is the ability to choose how you allocate your energy, attention, and time with clarity and conviction.*

Agency, however, requires trade-offs. This is where most redefinitions collapse. The world does not stand still while you craft a personal definition of success. It keeps scoring you by its own standards—productivity, prestige, speed. To live by an internal compass means risking the discomfort of being misunderstood. It means walking away from applause in pursuit of alignment. But the cost of conventional success is often steeper: chronic anxiety, emotional disconnection, and the slow erosion of authenticity. When the price of fitting in becomes the loss of yourself, the bargain is too expensive.

Take the example of Vicki Robin, co-author of *Your Money or Your Life*. Robin and her partner created a new metric for evaluating work: not income per hour, but *life energy expended per hour.* This recalibration allowed them to see how consumerism distorted their choices and to redesign life around purpose rather than paychecks. Their philosophy catalysed a movement—not because it told people to quit working, but because it illuminated a deeper truth: financial sufficiency is not about how much you earn, but how much freedom your relationship with money creates. That reframing—success as freedom, not accumulation—is now foundational to modern financial independence circles.

Similarly, among high-performing entrepreneurs, there's a growing movement away from "scale at all costs" towards "enough." Founders like Paul Jarvis, who wrote *Company of One*, advocate for businesses designed not to expand endlessly, but to sustain creativity and lifestyle alignment. In this model, success is not exponential revenue, but structural resilience—how well your business supports your life, not just your bank account. These examples suggest a radical idea: *you can be wildly successful by conventional standards and still fail at your own life*—unless you define success on your own terms and design accordingly.

One of the most insidious aspects of externally defined success is how it colonises your inner life. It rewards optimisation over reflection, scale over sustainability, urgency over depth. When your worth is tethered to performance, the result is chronic vigilance—never quite enough, never fully arrived. Psychological freedom begins when you decouple your identity from metrics you cannot control. That doesn't mean abandoning goals. It means contextualising them. Goals are useful servants, but dangerous masters. When your self-worth becomes contingent on milestones, you forfeit the sovereignty that success was meant to grant you.

This redefinition also requires grappling with the myth of linear progress. Life does not unfold like a career ladder or an S-curve. It loops, detours, unravels, and recomposes. Success, if it is to be lasting, must accommodate reinvention. Yet traditional success narratives treat pivots as failures, sabbaticals as indulgences, and ambiguity as weakness. In truth, these are signs of inner maturity. The ability to question your own definitions of success mid-stream—to ask whether the ladder you're climbing is still the right one—is a feature, not a flaw. It is a marker of wisdom, not instability.

In psychological terms, we might speak of "integrated ambition"—the desire to grow, achieve, and contribute, *while remaining in conversation with your values and limitations.* Integrated ambition differs from raw drive. It is more selective, more discerning, less reactive. It chooses where to exert effort, not just how much. It is success with depth. Without integration, ambition becomes extractive—pulling energy from every corner of your life without replenishment. With integration, ambition becomes regenerative—fuelled by alignment, coherence, and joy.

Of course, redefining success is not just personal—it is also political. When society elevates certain paths—white-collar careers, homeownership, elite education—as the default trajectory of success, it marginalises other forms of contribution. Care work, creative labour, community organising, spiritual leadership—these are often excluded from dominant success metrics, despite their profound societal value. A redefinition of success that does not question these hierarchies is incomplete. Equity requires expanding the lens—not just to include more people in success, but to expand what success means.

This expansion invites a shift in conversation from *what do you do* to *what do you value?* From *what have you built* to *how have you lived?* From *what have you accumulated* to *what have you nurtured, healed, or freed?* These are not sentimental questions. They are sovereign ones. Because ultimately, success is not a location, it's a *relation*—to your time, your self, your work, your community. To redefine it is to reclaim authorship over your life's arc.

This article does not ask you to reject ambition. It invites you to refine it. It does not condemn achievement. It interrogates its cost. And it does not offer a single new definition of success, but a discipline: the *ongoing, conscious articulation of your own metrics, aligned with your deepest values, revised as you evolve*. This is a success that adapts to complexity, honours your particularity, and grants you the rarest reward in a world of copy-paste ambition—*authentic freedom*.

The Currency of Conviction –

For most investors, conviction is conflated with confidence. The louder the belief, the more persuasive the pitch. But conviction, in its truest form, is not a performance—it is a currency. And like all valuable currencies, it holds its worth not in moments of consensus, but in moments of doubt. To invest with conviction is not to be bullish when others are bullish. It is to act with alignment when the world offers neither applause nor assurance. It is a form of long-term integrity—an economic expression of principle over popularity.

This form of conviction is especially rare in markets dominated by short-term metrics. Quarterly earnings, algorithmic trading, and viral narratives leave little space for principle-led positioning. Yet history consistently rewards those who dare to deviate—especially when their deviation is not arbitrary, but rooted in a coherent worldview. The great contrarians of finance and enterprise—people like John Templeton, Cathie Wood, Yvon Chouinard, and Paul Polman—weren't simply making bets against the herd. They were allocating capital in accordance with values that predated the trend. This is the essence of the currency of conviction: it is spendable *before* the crowd understands its value.

Consider the example of Rose Marcario, the former CEO of Patagonia. During her tenure, she made decisions that defied conventional capitalist logic. She reduced corporate growth targets in favour of environmental stewardship. She reinvested profits into activism, not just expansion. In 2018, she redirected a $10 million tax windfall into grassroots climate efforts. Wall Street analysts were baffled. But Patagonia's customer loyalty surged. So did its profitability. What seemed like ideological risk turned out to be brand strategy—because when conviction is real, it signals trust. And trust is a long-term asset that no spreadsheet can fully price.

The misunderstanding around conviction is that it must be loud to be credible. In reality, the strongest convictions are often quiet, sustained over decades, not quarters. Take John Bogle, founder of Vanguard, who in the 1970s introduced index funds to a market obsessed with active returns. At the time, his ideas were ridiculed. Competitors called passive investing "un-American." But Bogle wasn't trying to win favour. He was following a moral argument about fairness and investor protection. Today, index funds dominate global capital flows. His conviction—anchored in principle, executed with discipline—reshaped an industry.

What's crucial in these examples is not just the courage to stand alone, but the clarity to know *why*. Conviction divorced from principle becomes stubbornness. But conviction informed by coherent values becomes a force multiplier. It enables not just better decisions, but better resilience. Because when setbacks come—and they always do—it is not confidence that sustains you. It is the knowledge that you were acting from something deeper than fear or fashion.

This matters not only for capital allocators, but for anyone designing a life of intention. The currency of conviction is spendable in careers, relationships, and personal growth. To take a job aligned with your ethics, even if it pays less. To back a founder whose mission matches your worldview, even when the market wavers. To walk away from opportunities that look good on paper but feel hollow in the gut. These are all forms of investment. And their return is not just financial—it is existential. They build a life that feels internally consistent, not externally compliant.

Yet aligning investments with conviction often comes at a cost. You may lose short-term returns. You may alienate peers. You may endure long periods of being "wrong" before the market catches up. But the deeper cost lies in avoiding this alignment—living with the dull ache of compromise, the slow erosion of self-trust. Conviction requires trade-offs, but it also grants something rarer: the peace that comes from living in coherence with your own values.

There's a myth that conviction is inherently rigid. In reality, true conviction evolves. It is updated not through pressure, but through principled reflection. Consider the arc of Ray Dalio, founder of Bridgewater Associates. Known for his radical transparency and data-driven decision-making, Dalio also underwent a major philosophical shift after misjudging the 1982 market. He lost clients, credibility, and confidence. But instead of abandoning his core beliefs, he refined them—developing a system of open disagreement, systematic learning, and value-rooted investing. His conviction did not harden. It matured. This is the paradox: the strongest convictions are those most capable of intelligent adaptation.

There is, of course, a tension between conviction and consensus. The market, like society, rewards conformity—until it doesn't. When the tide turns, those who held fast to their principles are suddenly hailed as visionaries. But that moment of recognition often arrives too late to be useful. Conviction must therefore be its own reward. You invest in what you believe not because it's easy, but because it's necessary—for your integrity, for your clarity, for your legacy. If profit follows, so much the better. But the act itself has value, irrespective of outcome.

This applies equally to large institutional actors and individual investors. ESG investing, once seen as a niche, has become a trillion-dollar segment—not because it maximises returns in every quarter, but because it reflects a broader shift: the alignment of money with meaning. Still, the field is rife with performative gestures—greenwashing, diversity pledges without accountability, shallow mission statements. The currency of conviction demands more. It asks not how your portfolio looks, but how it *feels*. Not what box it checks, but what future it builds.

For founders, the principle is especially sharp. Building a company with conviction means embedding values into its DNA, not retrofitting them later. It means hiring, pricing, marketing, and product development all aligned with a central thesis about what matters. It means being willing to forgo certain customers, investors, or markets that conflict with your core beliefs. Again, the cost is real—but so is the moat. Purpose-led companies create loyalty that transactional competitors cannot replicate.

One striking case is that of Ben & Jerry's, whose founders famously refused to sell out their mission when Unilever acquired them. They negotiated an independent board to oversee the company's social mission, preserving their values post-acquisition. Critics called it naïve. Decades later, the brand's social credibility remains intact—arguably enhanced—precisely because that credibility was never for sale. This is the long tail of conviction: it may constrain you in the short term, but it compounds as reputational equity over time.

The currency of conviction is especially critical in times of disruption. When the world becomes volatile—economically, politically, socially—principles provide ballast. They allow you to move through uncertainty with purpose, rather than reaction. This is not to say that conviction guarantees success. Many who act from principle fail by conventional standards. But they do not suffer the deeper failure: misalignment with their own conscience. And that integrity, once lost, is rarely regained.

To cultivate this currency requires both introspection and articulation. You must know what you believe—and be able to express it, test it, defend it, and evolve it. This is not performative virtue. It is rigorous self-awareness. It is sitting with your own discomfort, your own blind spots, your own contradictions. It is choosing not the easy investment, but the meaningful one. And in doing so, building not just wealth, but wisdom.

Ultimately, the currency of conviction is measured not in dollars or metrics, but in the life you build. It is the kind of wealth that survives market crashes, career pivots, and public scrutiny. It is quiet, but unshakable. It does not always pay off in quarterly returns. But over time, it does something rarer: it compounds integrity. And in a world where compromise is cheap and noise is plentiful, that is a currency worth holding.

Decentralized Life Design –

The modern world, for all its promise of abundance, operates on brittle foundations. Fragile supply chains, institutional mistrust, algorithmically distorted incentives, and political volatility—these systemic instabilities have taught a new generation of thinkers a hard truth: resilience cannot be outsourced. To live freely in a world built on dependence is not freedom at all. *Decentralised life design is not a fringe philosophy—it is fast becoming a rational imperative.*

At its core, decentralised living is about engineering autonomy by design, not by chance. It does not require rejecting modern systems wholesale, but it does require confronting the illusion that they will always work in your favour. The decentralised life is not anti-institutional—it is post-institutional. It asks: what happens when your most essential needs—income, housing, education, mobility, even meaning—are no longer outsourced to fragile external systems, but reconfigured to live closer to your values and within your circle of control?

For decades, society equated progress with specialisation and interdependence. In theory, this division of labour created efficiency. In practice, it created asymmetry: institutions gained scale while individuals lost sovereignty. The 2008 financial crisis, the COVID-19 pandemic, and the crumbling of trust in centralised systems—from health to education to governance—have punctured the myth of stability. In its place, a quieter movement has emerged: *not of panic or paranoia, but of design.* People are no longer waiting for systems to change. They are building alternative architectures.

A decentralised life begins with rethinking dependence. Consider the most basic structure of modern life: employment. For many, a single job provides income, identity, insurance, and often housing or location. This is not diversification—it is concentration risk masquerading as security. In a decentralised model, income is layered. A writer may teach online, license intellectual property, and consult independently. A craftsman might sell directly, run workshops, and host events. This modularity is not just about economics; it is psychological. *When no single node holds all your power, you regain optionality.*

Optionality underpins the decentralised ethos. The goal is not total independence—an unrealistic and often isolating fantasy—but *flexible interdependence*, where no node—employer, platform, bank, government—is a single point of failure. Consider the way decentralised finance (DeFi) models emerged—not to destroy central banks, but to create parallel systems where access, privacy, and ownership were not granted by institutional gatekeepers but coded into the architecture. The analogy extends to life: what if your healthcare, learning, mobility, and earning systems were built with local resilience, ethical alignment, and redundancy in mind?

Minimalism is often misunderstood as aesthetic austerity. In decentralised life design, it becomes a tactical strategy—*reducing reliance, not merely reducing possessions*. When one owns less, one insures less, maintains less, and fears less. This allows for faster mobility, lower overhead, and greater adaptability. In a world defined by volatility, this is not monkish detachment—it is practical resilience.

This mindset is increasingly visible in how people structure their housing and geography. The rise of location-independent living is not simply a tech-enabled luxury; it's a response to systemic failure—rising rents, hollowed-out cities, and exclusionary property markets. Some choose mobile lifestyles not as wanderers, but as *strategic generalists*. Others build community housing cooperatives, off-grid eco-villages, or land trusts that restore agency to the local level. Each of these is a decentralisation of the housing function—one less link in the institutional chain.

The same logic applies to education. Legacy education systems, with their credential inflation and debt traps, are losing credibility. In their place, decentralised alternatives are thriving: self-directed learning, cohort-based courses, skill-based micro-certifications, and intergenerational mentorships. These forms reimagine learning as continuous, contextual, and personally governed. In this model, *learning is not downloaded from authority—it is designed for utility.*

Yet decentralised life design does not mean doing everything alone. In fact, it often requires more community, not less. Peer networks, knowledge circles, time-banks, mutual aid systems, and micro-entrepreneurship hubs are the social infrastructure of post-institutional living. When institutions fail to serve their purpose, people don't retreat into isolation—they reorganise in smaller, tighter formations. *Decentralisation doesn't diminish society—it reconfigures it.*

The psychological dimension cannot be ignored. For many, institutional reliance offers not just comfort, but identity. Detaching from that is not simply a technical challenge—it's an existential one. Decentralised living demands inner sovereignty: the ability to trust one's own discernment in a world that rewards conformity. It asks: whose voice defines success? Whose metrics are you optimising for? The person designing their own life system must not only be a strategist—but also a steward of their inner compass.

Resilience, in this sense, is both external and internal. It's not enough to build systems that survive volatility; one must also *train for ambiguity*. A decentralised life is not a bunker—it is an experiment in agency. It replaces institutional guarantees with personal adaptability, static roles with dynamic reinvention. Those who thrive in this environment are not just hedging—they're learning to live in flow with change.

Real-world case studies reflect this shift. Entrepreneurs like Naval Ravikant advocate for self-sovereignty through leverage—code, capital, and media that compound independently of institutional permission. Investors like Tim Ferriss structure portfolios not just for returns but for freedom of time and attention. Communities like Zomia or Start9 reimagine digital and physical infrastructure from the ground up—rooted in ethical autonomy and decentralised governance. These are not fringe actors—they are early adopters of a different design principle.

There are, of course, trade-offs. Decentralisation is not utopia. It demands intentionality, continuous learning, and an appetite for uncertainty. Systems that are decentralised are harder to scale, harder to regulate, and often slower to standardise. But they are also harder to corrupt, harder to monopolise, and less prone to catastrophic collapse. *What you lose in ease, you gain in antifragility.*

The question, then, is not whether decentralised life design is better—it is whether it is necessary. As the reliability of traditional institutions continues to degrade, the burden of sovereignty shifts. Those who wait for systems to change may be waiting forever. Those who begin designing lives that function independently of fragile scaffolding are not rebelling—they are rehearsing for reality.

Ultimately, decentralised life design is not about escape. It is about alignment. It's about designing a life where your values are expressed not only in what you believe, but in *how you live.* It is about seeing every dependency as a decision, every habit as a vote for a system, every structure as a tool or a trap. It invites the reader not to withdraw from society, but to rewire it—quietly, purposefully, and from the inside out. Not to opt out, but to build better. One decision at a time.

Becoming the Trustee of Your Own Life –

Ownership is often reduced to possession—of wealth, property, or titles. But true ownership, in its most evolved form, is not about control. It is about *custodianship.* It asks not what you own, but what you are responsible for. To become the trustee of your own life is to adopt a deeper orientation: one where your time, energy, attention, relationships, and resources are seen not as mere assets, but as a trust you are ethically bound to steward—intentionally, wisely, and with integrity.

This reframing is not rhetorical. It has teeth. In law, a trustee is someone who holds assets not for their own benefit, but for the long-term well-being of another. Apply this idea to yourself, and a radical proposition emerges: *You are both the beneficiary and the trustee of your life.* You are tasked with managing your most precious resources—your focus, your years, your principles—not for instant gratification, but for the continuity and coherence of your deepest values across time.

Most people operate their lives as though they are temporary tenants, not long-term trustees. They rent their time to employers, defer their convictions to peer norms, and invest their energy reactively. This is not a moral failure—it is a cultural inheritance. Industrial society rewarded obedience and optimisation, not sovereignty. The tragedy is not only in the misallocation of resources, but in the erosion of *interior governance*. Sovereignty begins not with money, but with mindset. And the most mature form of sovereignty is not self-indulgence, but self-stewardship.

Consider time. We speak of "spending" it, "wasting" it, occasionally "saving" it. Rarely do we talk about *investing* time as a fiduciary act on behalf of our future self. If we did, our calendars would look radically different. We would guard our mornings not out of productivity fetishism, but because the first hours of attention shape the entire arc of meaning. We would prioritise recovery, reflection, and solitude—not as luxuries, but as responsibilities. The trustee of their life does not outsource their schedule to algorithms, nor their aspirations to social scripts.

The same principle applies to values. In an ownership culture dominated by external metrics—status, scale, visibility—many people lose the plot of what they actually stand for. To become a trustee is to ask, without irony or evasion: *What do I hold sacred?* What am I here to protect, preserve, extend? These are not rhetorical questions. They shape real behaviours. A trustee who values creative freedom may reject lucrative offers that compromise voice. One who values intergenerational healing may spend years reparenting their own patterns before raising children. Trusteeship is not performative. It is deeply quiet. But it alters everything.

Legacy, in this light, becomes an active discipline. Not a posthumous inheritance, but a visible trail of integrity. Legacy is built not at the finish line, but in *daily micro-allocations*: what you prioritise, what you postpone, what you protect. The trustee understands that their time on this earth is finite, but their influence is not. Each act of alignment plants seeds. Each choice not to conform becomes a future branch. In this sense, to live as a trustee is to play a *longer game than your lifespan*. The work is not only personal—it is ancestral and architectural.

Real-world examples of this ethos are everywhere—though often understated. Patagonia's founder Yvon Chouinard didn't sell his company for personal gain; he transferred ownership to a trust and a nonprofit committed to climate preservation. The decision wasn't merely philanthropic. It reflected a belief that *value is what endures when control is relinquished for purpose.* His trusteeship was both financial and moral. Similarly, the late Toni Morrison once said she wrote "in order to be a good ancestor." Not a brand. Not a celebrity. A *literary steward*, accountable to lineage, not algorithms.

Contrast this with modern culture's obsession with optimisation. The productivity industrial complex encourages people to treat their lives as harvest cycles: squeeze as much as possible from every minute, monetise every passion, expand every platform. But this is extractive thinking masquerading as efficiency. Trusteeship suggests a different paradigm—*regenerative stewardship.* The point is not to maximise every resource, but to tend to it so that it remains healthy, whole, and capable of growing without burnout or collapse.

This distinction matters deeply in an age of burnout, distraction, and disillusionment. If you are the trustee of your own life, your role is not to exploit yourself in service of external rewards. It is to caretake the coherence of your identity across time. What remains consistent across your decisions? What principles animate your pivots? What line, if any, do you refuse to cross—even when no one is watching? These questions cannot be answered in performance mode. They require stillness. Discernment. Sometimes, they require loss.

Because trusteeship is costly. It asks for restraint in a culture of indulgence. It asks for reflection in a culture of noise. It requires that you say no to things you could easily justify saying yes to. It might cost you opportunities, applause, even relationships. But it protects something far rarer: *alignment.* And over the long arc of a life, alignment compounds in a way that approval never can.

There is also a communal aspect to trusteeship. Though it begins with individual agency, it does not end in isolation. To live as a trustee is to be accountable not just to yourself, but to others—peers, elders, descendants, even strangers whose lives you may never touch directly. Trusteeship recognises that our choices are not contained.

They ripple. They shape norms, economies, ecosystems, and expectations. What we tolerate, others normalise. What we question, others consider. Trustees are not just architects of their own legacy—they are *cultural carriers* of possibility.

This is why stewardship of voice matters. In a time when misinformation spreads faster than truth, and authenticity is often weaponised for brand value, the trustee is careful. They do not publish everything they think, nor perform every identity they explore. Their speech is not repressed—but *responsible.* They understand that their credibility is not a personal trophy; it is a public trust. What they say shapes what becomes sayable.

And perhaps the most radical act of trusteeship is the decision to *reimagine success*. Not as scale, dominance, or visibility—but as inner coherence. A life where the external reflects the internal. Where success is measured by *fit*, not comparison. This is not a retreat from ambition. It is a relocation of ambition from status to significance. From fleeting relevance to enduring resonance. A trustee is not afraid of scale, but they do not conflate it with impact. They know that legacy begins when leverage meets conscience.

Ultimately, becoming the trustee of your own life is not a self-help slogan. It is a civic stance. A spiritual contract. A managerial philosophy. It redefines ownership as ethical agency—across time, across relationships, across systems. And while it demands more from us than passive existence ever could, it offers something that passive existence never will: the chance to be proud not just of what we did, but of *how we lived.*

Conclusion
The Quiet Revolution

The transformation this book has advocated is less about tactics than orientation—a subtle, yet profound, rethinking of money, ownership, and meaning. Previous chapters challenged assumptions and introduced practical shifts; this final chapter invites a bolder proposition: to become wealth itself. Not merely to possess it, but to embody it—to be a vessel through which value flows because one is anchored, deliberate, and aligned. Paradoxically, the more wealth is internalised as a mode of being, the less one feels compelled to display it, and the more organically it multiplies.

Much of modern life revolves around extraction: extracting value from time, relationships, even from oneself. The quiet revolution lies in pivoting from extraction to expression. It is the difference between asking, "What can I gain?" and asking, "What am I here to offer?"—not in a moralistic sense, but in a grounded, owner-conscious way. A person who has authored their values, sharpened their attention, and chosen their boundaries no longer chases wealth—they become it.

This is not metaphorical. Internal capacity—emotional range, discernment, adaptability, alignment—is the rarest currency. It cannot be inherited or commodified. And yet, it amplifies every other form of wealth. Emotional self-regulation improves investment decisions. Tolerance for ambiguity mitigates panic during market volatility. Leading with principles generates sustainable influence. When psychological sovereignty is paired with financial means, wealth multiplies exponentially.

Becoming wealth requires living in tension with cultural noise. Society still glorifies external markers: net worth, prestige, productivity, scale. Speed is sold as efficiency, scale as significance. Quiet success—borne of integrity, reflection, and deliberate choice—rarely captures attention. And that is precisely the point: a quiet revolution moves under the surface, reshaping the ground, not seeking applause.

One of the most striking insights is that financial independence is not a terminus—it is a threshold. Once survival is secured and leverage earned, deeper questions emerge: What now? What is worth building when compulsion is removed? What should be preserved when no one is forcing your hand? How do your decisions shape the future—whether in business, family, citizenship, or culture? Viewing surplus as creative capacity transforms the actor: less reactive, more intentional.

Legacy, therefore, cannot be postponed. It is not confined to wills or end-of-life planning; it is embedded in how power is wielded, how presence is felt, how decisions are made when no observer exists. Legacy is authored in moments, not milestones. To craft it well demands full engagement—intellect, ambition, clarity, curiosity, and courage.

Consider the "financial imprint": the patterns, norms, and values embedded in daily choices. Most inherit these from family or culture, consciously or otherwise. Few are taught to edit or reframe them. Yet once we recognise the script, we can choose to replicate it—or reinvent it. The quiet revolution begins here, with authorship over inherited financial and emotional narratives.

Reinvention need not be grandiose. It thrives in small, repeatable acts: choosing transparency over posturing, prioritising long-term relationships over short-term gain, redefining "enough" in a world obsessed with excess, investing in learning for liberation rather than signalling. Each micro-act is an assertion of sovereignty. Repetition creates momentum; momentum becomes culture—personal, familial, generational.

A common misconception is that mastery lies in control. In reality, it lies in clarity. Control is rigid; clarity is adaptive. A clear mind discerns which risks are strategic, which trade-offs matter, which doors must close to maintain alignment. Clarity tolerates uncertainty, grounded not in perfection but discernment. Those with clarity act decisively amid ambiguity—not grasping, but guiding.

Psychological freedom is as crucial as financial freedom. Without it, money traps: fuel for insecurity, a tool for validation, a shield against fear. With it, money becomes leverage—an instrument of expression, stewardship, and selective impact. Most financial education stops at spreadsheets. Yet spreadsheets alone cannot craft a life worth living; for that, philosophy, narrative, and context are essential.

Integration requires rhythm—a cyclical return to core principles. Simplicity, for instance, may manifest as minimalism in one decade, selective excellence in the next, and intentional succession planning later still. Principles, refracted through time, build a wealth philosophy that matures alongside its owner.

The path forward is not singular, but there are anchors: values should precede velocity; freedom without responsibility masks fragility; ownership requires courage to release; alignment is a more reliable compass than ambition. These are invitations—to pause, to inquire, to choose again.

The revolution is quiet because it does not need spectacle. It unfolds in decisions rather than declarations, in calendars rather than quotations, shaped by those who refuse to outsource power, betray values, or equate optimisation with wisdom. Such individuals may not always be understood, but they command respect—from anyone who recognises sovereignty when it enters a room.

The ultimate act of ownership is not acquisition; it is authorship. To cease imitation and begin design. To see life not as reaction but as canvas, where constraints are opportunities and choices are intentional strokes. Whether at the start of a career, amid family responsibilities, or contemplating exit, the invitation remains: steward your time, attention, relationships, capital, and voice with seriousness.

Enduring wealth is not measured by accumulation but by contribution. It is not merely what one leaves behind, but what is shaped in the present. Thinking like an owner—of meaning, agency, and assets—transforms life itself. And if enough embrace this responsibility quietly, rigorously, and consistently, the quiet revolution will inevitably make itself known.

Becoming Wealth, Not Just Having It –

For much of modern economic thought, wealth has been defined as accumulation—of assets, of options, of insulation against risk. The archetype is straightforward: the wealthy person has more. More money. More property. More freedom to say no. But this definition, while functionally accurate, is spiritually thin. It describes *what* wealth is but says nothing about *who* becomes wealthy in a deeper, more embodied sense. To truly think like an owner—of capital, of self, of life—we must interrogate not just the metrics of wealth but the identity of it. The more transformative question is not, *How much do I have?* but *Who do I become by having it?*

To become wealth is to develop internal capacities that persist regardless of external fluctuations. This is not an idealistic abstraction. It is a measurable shift in how people relate to uncertainty, choice, influence, and contribution. A person who has cultivated discernment, groundedness, and a capacity for long-term thinking has something that no market crash can erase. The rise and fall of capital may affect their liquidity, but it does not dictate their identity. *Wealth, then, is not merely stored in balance sheets; it is embedded in character.*

This transformation is not automatic. Many people with high net worths remain psychologically impoverished—chronically anxious, reactive, validation-seeking. They fear losing what they've acquired because they haven't integrated it into who they are. They are *owners* on paper, but renters in mindset—dependent on the external to prop up a fragile internal narrative. Conversely, others with comparatively modest means can move through life with clarity, agency, and creative authority. The difference lies not in possession, but in integration. *Becoming wealth means the outer reflects the inner, not compensates for its absence.*

Consider the distinction between extraction and cultivation. Accumulating wealth through extraction—of time, labour, status—is common. But cultivation implies something different: a relationship to wealth that is participatory and generative. It means building capacities like patience, emotional range, and strategic empathy. These aren't typically taught in financial education, yet they determine the sustainability of wealth far more than any technical portfolio strategy. For example, family offices that last generations tend to focus as much on the emotional intelligence of heirs as on fiduciary mechanics. Because they understand the truth: *unprocessed psychology is one of the greatest risks to capital.*

When people pursue external wealth without internal development, they tend to amplify their existing patterns—good or bad. A scarcity mindset becomes magnified by money, not erased. So does impulsivity, ego, avoidance. What was once a personal quirk becomes a systemic vulnerability. This is why becoming wealth demands self-inquiry: *What drives my decisions when no one is watching? What parts of me am I trying to soothe through spending, acquiring, or giving?* Without this introspection, even philanthropy can become a performance—more about optics than authentic alignment.

The shift from having to becoming is best illustrated through lived example. Consider the case of entrepreneur-turned-investor Naval Ravikant. In interviews, he has repeatedly drawn a line between financial success and peace of mind, arguing that the latter is the more difficult and important wealth to attain. His emphasis on leverage, clarity, and optionality isn't just tactical—it's philosophical. The real wealth, he suggests, is freedom from compulsion. Similarly, Vicki Robin, co-author of *Your Money or Your Life*, reframed wealth as the alignment between one's life energy and one's values. These are not fringe thinkers; they represent a growing cohort who see *being* as a financial competency.

There is also a cultural layer to this transformation. Traditional economic models are built on utility and competition. But the practice of becoming wealth shifts the focus toward stewardship and meaning. This is not antithetical to success—it is its maturation. Many second-generation wealth holders now speak openly about the psychological pressure of inheritance: the identity confusion, the guilt, the sense of displacement. What they often seek is not more but *coherence*—a sense that their financial power can be expressed in ways that feel congruent with their lived values. That, too, is part of becoming wealth: re-authoring narratives that were once passively inherited.

The future of financial education must reflect this shift. It cannot be reduced to investment vehicles and tax strategies. It must incorporate narrative literacy, emotional fluency, and ethical reflection. Because the person who understands their inner landscape can navigate complex decisions without being hijacked by ego or fear. They can sit with ambiguity, delay gratification, and choose the meaningful over the urgent. These are not soft skills; they are structural advantages. They enable better partnerships, more coherent leadership, and long-term resilience. *Becoming wealth is about becoming someone whose presence is an asset.*

The implications are not merely personal—they are institutional. Organisations led by individuals who embody this form of wealth tend to operate differently. They build cultures that reward integrity over short-term performance. They design systems that account for the whole human, not just the role. And they invest in ideas not just because they are profitable, but because they are principled. Patagonia's founder, Yvon Chouinard, famously gave away his company to a trust dedicated to climate sustainability—not as a sacrifice, but as a logical extension of his values. His wealth became an instrument of authorship.

This reframing challenges some deeply held assumptions about ownership itself. Ownership is often associated with control. But mature ownership looks more like stewardship. It is not about hoarding power, but about directing it wisely. It is not about permanence, but about purposeful transition. Becoming wealth means understanding that you are not just holding money—you are shaping ecosystems. Whether that ecosystem is your family, your organisation, or your community, your internal clarity becomes the governance model others feel.

The practical question, then, is: *How do we cultivate this internal capacity?* There is no one-size-fits-all answer. But certain practices are consistently effective. Stillness is one. Not as a luxury, but as a discipline that allows for deeper listening. Reflection is another—not in the abstract, but tied to actual decisions. Why did I say yes to that partnership? What was I avoiding when I made that investment? These questions turn money into a mirror, revealing the deeper motivations at play. Over time, this creates coherence. And *coherence is the most underrated form of confidence.*

Another practice is constraint. Deliberately choosing limitations that sharpen focus and prevent drift. This might look like capping lifestyle inflation even when earnings increase. Or setting thematic boundaries on what types of investments you'll pursue. These are not rules for the sake of austerity—they are architectures for clarity. In a world of endless options, constraint is a form of respect. For time, for values, for purpose. It signals that you are not just reacting to opportunity, but authoring a life with discernment.

To become wealth is ultimately to live a life that feels internally consistent, externally expressed, and sustainably aligned. It is to collapse the gap between what you believe and how you behave. Between what you say and what you fund. Between who you are and what your resources enable in the world. This is not a utopian ideal. It is a rigorous, daily practice. One that requires courage, self-awareness, and a willingness to evolve.

You are not merely an owner of capital. You are a creator of culture. A designer of norms. A transmitter of values. And whether you are building a business, leading a family, or shaping a personal legacy, the most enduring contribution you can make is not what you accumulated, but *who you became in the process.*

This is what it means to move from having wealth to becoming it. From counting numbers to crafting meaning. From reacting to designing. From extraction to expression. This is the heart of thinking like an owner—not of static assets, but of dynamic potential. And it is an identity no market correction can take away.

What You Leave Behind –

What endures when you're no longer in the room—your reputation, your principles, your influence—is a far more consequential measure of your life's worth than any line on a ledger. Yet legacy is often approached too late, too shallowly, or too mechanically. It's reduced to wills and estate plans, a portfolio left behind rather than a vision carried forward. But the deeper truth is that everyone, regardless of net worth, leaves something behind. The question is not *if*, but *what.* Legacy is not the luxury of the ultra-wealthy—it's the unavoidable imprint of how we've chosen to live.

The paradox of legacy is that while it is defined by the future, it is authored in the present. Most people postpone thinking about what they'll leave behind until their later years, assuming it to be a retirement-era concern. But by that time, the habits have hardened, the relationships have calcified, and the opportunities to shape culture—within family, business, or community—are diminished. To live with an awareness of legacy is not to fixate on death; it is to elevate life to a level of intentionality that most people never reach. *The most powerful legacies are not built at the end—they're lived in real time.*

One of the most sobering exercises any thoughtful person can do is to ask: *If I disappeared tomorrow, what would remain because of me?* Not just the possessions or accomplishments, but the values instilled, the relationships shaped, the standards normalised. Did you build systems that outlast your presence? Did you model ways of thinking that others now carry? Did you alter trajectories—financially, emotionally, ethically—for those within your sphere of influence?

In family contexts, legacy often gets filtered through material inheritance. Yet every advisor worth their salt will tell you: money passed without meaning often creates confusion, conflict, or dependence. Family office consultants report that the primary reason wealth fails to persist past the third generation is not market volatility or tax mismanagement—it's a lack of shared vision. Without clarity around *why* the family does what it does, money becomes inert, or worse, corrosive. By contrast, when values are codified—through stories, practices, governance structures—the assets gain narrative gravity. *Legacy, in this light, is less about transmission of capital and more about transference of consciousness.*

This is where the idea of intentional authorship becomes central. Every day, consciously or not, we are writing the story others will tell about us. Not the mythologised version polished by obituary editors, but the lived reality embedded in the memories and decisions of those we affect. That story is shaped by how we handle power, how we resolve tension, how we show up under pressure, how we invest not only our money but our time, our attention, and our energy. You don't need to be a founder or philanthropist to leave a lasting legacy. You just need to make your principles visible, repeatable, and resilient.

Take, for example, the life of Fred Swaniker, the Ghanaian entrepreneur who founded the African Leadership Academy and the African Leadership University. His legacy is not just institutional—it is philosophical. He recognised that leadership in Africa needed to be redefined, not just funded. By investing in character formation, strategic thinking, and pan-African identity, he has created ripple effects that far exceed his personal presence. The schools he built may evolve, but the mindset he has seeded is embedded in thousands of future decision-makers. *That is intentional authorship at scale.*

Yet authorship is not limited to monumental achievements. It can show up in the fidelity of daily actions. A mother who consistently models financial boundaries teaches her children that saying no is not scarcity but stewardship. A manager who speaks truth in uncomfortable meetings models courage as a cultural norm. A colleague who names ethical tension rather than glossing over it raises the baseline for integrity. These small acts, repeated over time, become scripts others internalise. They don't need to be remembered to be felt.

The challenge is that most people are not aware they're leaving a legacy while it's happening. They are busy, distracted, or unconsciously repeating inherited behaviours without examining their impact. That is why a practice of reflection is so essential—not in a vague, self-help way, but as a rigorous tool for authorship. Questions like: *What do I want to be known for in this context? What patterns am I reinforcing through my choices? What am I normalising without meaning to?* These are not rhetorical. They are the architecture of meaning. They guide not just how we act, but how others interpret our actions.

There is a practical dimension to this too. Authors of legacy often invest in artefacts—tools that preserve meaning beyond proximity. This can include letters to future generations, family constitutions, value-aligned trusts, endowments that fund specific missions, or business exit strategies that ensure the enterprise lives according to original principles. What matters is not the medium, but the intentionality behind it. These artefacts become anchors, giving shape to what might otherwise dissipate.

Of course, intentionality without humility becomes control. Some people try to micromanage their legacy from the grave, dictating how money must be spent or how successors must behave. This usually backfires. It signals mistrust and narrows possibility. The more effective approach is one of *co-authorship*—inviting the next generation into dialogue, giving them context, but leaving room for evolution. The best legacies are adaptable. They honour the original vision while allowing reinterpretation. Think of them not as monuments but as living frameworks. *A legacy should feel like a foundation, not a fortress.*

This tension—between authorship and release—is perhaps the most sophisticated financial and philosophical challenge there is. It asks us to take responsibility for our influence without clinging to control. It calls for foresight, but also flexibility. And it requires that we shift from metrics to meaning. The return on investment here is not measured in basis points, but in the character and capability of those who inherit our systems, assets, and stories.

Ultimately, the question of *what you leave behind* is not separate from how you live—it is the echo of it. The decisions you make when no one is watching, the standards you hold when expedience tempts, the moments you elevate values over outcomes—these all accrue. Not in headlines or eulogies, but in the undercurrents of how others navigate their own lives because of you. Whether you are shaping a company culture, a family ethos, or a personal philosophy, the imperative is the same: *author with intent, live with consistency, and leave with clarity.*

Because the most enduring legacies are not built through wealth transfer, but through value transmission. They do not reside in bank accounts, but in behavioural norms. They are not remembered because they were dramatic, but because they were dependable. You don't have to predict what the world will become—you just need to stand clearly enough in what you believe that others can orient around it when you're no longer there.

What you leave behind is not the sum of what you acquired, but the net impact of what you stood for, repeated, and modelled. And when you live from that awareness—daily, deliberately—you are no longer preparing for legacy. You are already living it.

The Path Forward –

The end of a book is rarely the end of its influence—at least, not when the content was never designed to be a prescription, but a provocation. If you've read this far, the most important question is not whether you've agreed with every idea, but whether you've begun to think more actively, deliberately, and independently about your own financial philosophy. The final chapter is not a summation. It is a recalibration point—a pivot from assimilation to application. And like all true wisdom, the ideas that endure are not those you merely understand, but those you revisit. *The real test of insight is its utility over time.*

Too often, we treat personal finance as a series of finish lines: hit a number, acquire a home, pay off the debt, retire early. But this mindset reinforces a one-dimensional narrative that fails to account for the evolving nature of human identity. What served you in your twenties may constrain you in your forties. A principle that helped you grow may later require unlearning. The path forward, then, is not paved with fixed rules but with flexible anchors—ideas strong enough to return to, yet adaptable enough to meet you at new levels of maturity.

One such anchor is the concept of *enough.* At every stage of life, the definition of enough must be interrogated. Not in abstract terms, but in precise, context-specific language. What is enough income for this season? Enough risk? Enough external validation? Most people outsource this question to cultural norms or peer comparison. But a deeply examined "enough" liberates you from the tyranny of endless striving. It introduces boundary and dignity into ambition. It allows for desire without delusion. When regularly revisited, it becomes a compass for right-sizing your financial decisions against your evolving reality.

A second enduring principle is *alignment over optimisation.* Much of modern financial advice is obsessed with efficiency—lowest fees, highest returns, fastest paths. But a purely optimised life can easily become one that is technically impressive and emotionally vacant. Alignment, by contrast, asks harder questions: does this investment align with my values? Does this income source cost me more than it gives? Does my calendar reflect what I claim to prioritise? Alignment sacrifices a bit of performance for a lot of coherence. And over the long arc of a life, coherence produces a more durable form of satisfaction than perfection ever could.

Another principle worth revisiting is *ownership as stewardship.* In early stages, ownership often centres on control—controlling your income, schedule, environment. As one matures, however, the lens widens: ownership is not merely about possession, but about responsibility. Stewardship reframes what you have—whether time, capital, influence—not as entitlements but as entrusted assets. This principle grows in potency with age. A young professional may apply it by choosing impact-driven work. A parent may interpret it through intergenerational teaching. A retiree may act on it by shaping philanthropic commitments. Regardless of stage, stewardship shifts the focus from "What can I extract?" to "What am I responsible for preserving or evolving?"

In practice, these principles are not meant to constrain creativity but to frame reflection. Life, after all, does not unfold linearly. You will revisit seasons of uncertainty, ambition, contraction, and reinvention. A job loss may feel like regression, but it could be a catalytic realignment. A financial windfall may invite expansion, but also require inner recalibration. The temptation in these moments is to grab for new frameworks, to change everything. But often the wiser path is to return—not to what's comfortable, but to what's foundational. To use these enduring principles as touchstones, not checklists.

Consider the story of Vicki Robin, co-author of *Your Money or Your Life*, who reached financial independence decades before FIRE became a movement. Her lifestyle wasn't flashy or viral—it was intentional. What makes her example powerful is not just the mechanics of frugality, but the philosophy that guided her: money is life energy. That framing allowed her to reassess decisions again and again, across changing stages of life, without betraying the core insight. Her "path forward" was not a straight line but a spiral—revisiting, refining, recommitting.

Or take the late Paul Polman, former CEO of Unilever, who famously refused to give quarterly guidance to Wall Street, believing it fostered short-termism. That decision was not just strategic, but principled. He redefined what success looked like in corporate leadership by anchoring to values of sustainability and long-term impact. The principle—*profit without purpose is hollow*—didn't expire with his tenure. It lives on in the policies, expectations, and market conversations that his stance helped reframe. That's the power of timeless ideas: they outlast the moment that made them necessary.

For individuals designing their path forward, it's critical to distinguish between principles and preferences. Preferences shift. They are shaped by mood, social pressure, convenience. Principles endure precisely because they resist those tides. Yet they must not become dogma. The goal is to hold them firmly but flexibly—to keep them alive through reinterpretation. As you age, for example, your risk appetite may decline, but your principle of autonomy may remain. You might translate it from financial independence into spatial freedom or intellectual sovereignty. The core value stays; the application evolves.

This chapter, then, is not offering new frameworks. It's asking you to internalise a meta-framework: *live in a way that allows you to continually return to what matters most, with deeper clarity and more refined action each time.* That means building margin into your financial plans—not just emergency funds, but bandwidth for change. It means documenting your reasoning—not only your numbers—so that future-you understands past-you's logic. It means curating information diets, peer groups, and mentors that reinforce rather than distract from your core direction.

There's also a broader cultural implication to embracing timeless principles. In a world built on the economics of novelty, stillness becomes a kind of rebellion. The ability to remain anchored while others chase the next trend is not stagnation—it is sovereignty. Timelessness is not about being outdated; it is about becoming unmoved by distraction. And in that stillness, there is power—the power to act rather than react, to design rather than drift.

A final observation: the more secure someone becomes in their principles, the more generous they tend to be. Not just financially, but emotionally, intellectually, and relationally. People who revisit and refine their values over time tend to see life not as a competitive race, but as a cooperative continuum. They invest in others, teach without ego, and contribute to systems they may never benefit from directly. This form of wealth—the generative kind—is what often makes a life feel well-lived. It is the quiet yield of having chosen to walk the path forward with intention rather than impulse.

Ultimately, the most enduring lives are not those packed with novelty, but those scaffolded by insight. And the most powerful insights are not those that promise immediate transformation, but those that invite lifelong interrogation. This book was never meant to answer every question. It was designed to leave you with better questions—questions that keep revealing new layers as you grow. The path forward is yours to shape. But you never have to shape it alone. Return to the ideas that clarify, to the principles that calm, to the voices that challenge without confusing. Revisit. Reaffirm. Reinvent. And walk on.

About the Author

Julian Hawthorne is a disciplined thinker and wealth mindset specialist, drawing on years of study in behavioral finance, Stoic philosophy, and generational legacy-building. His work guides readers beyond conventional money advice toward cultivating the inner architecture of financial resilience and purpose. With a background rooted in both qualitative research and real-world mentorship, Julian shows how shifting identity and decision frameworks unlock transformative, enduring wealth. — Aligns seamlessly with the intellectual, emotional, and philosophical depth of Think Like an Owner.

www.ingramcontent.com/pod-product-compliance
Lightning Source LLC
Chambersburg PA
CBHW031348230926
51848CB00002B/429
* 9 7 8 9 3 7 1 7 7 8 2 0 6 *